Getting Started with the Lazarus IDE

Get to grips with the basics of programming, debugging, creating, and documenting projects with the Lazarus IDE

Roderick Person

[PACKT] open source*
PUBLISHING   community experience distilled

BIRMINGHAM - MUMBAI

Getting Started with the Lazarus IDE

Copyright © 2013 Packt Publishing

First published: February 2013

Production Reference: 1180213

Published by Packt Publishing Ltd.
Livery Place
35 Livery Street
Birmingham B3 2PB, UK.

ISBN 978-1-78216-340-4

www.packtpub.com

Cover Image by Asher Wishkerman (wishkerman@hotmail.com)

Credits

Author
Roderick Person

Reviewer
Juha Manninen

Acquisition Editor
Rukhsana Khambatta

Commissioning Editor
Ameya Sawant

Technical Editors
Kaustubh S. Mayekar

Shruti Sugunan

Dominic Pereira

Copy Editor
Brandt D'Mello

Project Coordinator
Joel Goveya

Proofreader
Lauren Tobon

Indexer
Hemangini Bari

Production Coordinator
Pooja Chiplunkar

Cover Work
Pooja Chiplunkar

About the Author

Roderick Person has a varied background in the corporate IT field. For the last 14 years, he has been a programmer for one of the top-ranked health system in the United States. He is experienced with developing applications in Delphi, Free Pascal, Python, SQL, and other languages. He is also an advocate of leveraging open source applications in a corporate environment.

I'd like to thank Barbara Kolski for her support and encouragement with this book, and my wife, Vicky Starr, and daughter, Milan Starr.

About the Reviewer

Juha Manninen is a software developer with more than 25 years of experience. Now, as a middle-aged man, he is studying in a university of applied sciences.

He has been a part of the Lazarus development team since 2009. However, as the team is made up of developers who volunteer their time to the project without compensation, Juha earns a living as a Delphi programmer.

Object Pascal is his favorite programming language, because it's a nice combination of native-compiled code and clear syntax.

www.PacktPub.com

Support files, eBooks, discount offers and more

You might want to visit www.PacktPub.com for support files and downloads related to your book.

Did you know that Packt offers eBook versions of every book published, with PDF and ePub files available? You can upgrade to the eBook version at www.PacktPub.com and as a print book customer, you are entitled to a discount on the eBook copy. Get in touch with us at service@packtpub.com for more details.

At www.PacktPub.com, you can also read a collection of free technical articles, sign up for a range of free newsletters and receive exclusive discounts and offers on Packt books and eBooks.

http://PacktLib.PacktPub.com

Do you need instant solutions to your IT questions? PacktLib is Packt's online digital book library. Here, you can access, read, and search across Packt's entire library of books.

Why Subscribe?

- Fully searchable across every book published by Packt
- Copy and paste, print, and bookmark content
- On demand and accessible via web browser

Free Access for Packt account holders

If you have an account with Packt at www.PacktPub.com, you can use this to access PacktLib today and view nine entirely free books. Simply use your login credentials for immediate access.

Table of Contents

Preface

Lazarus is an open-source integrated development environment for the Free Pascal compiler. Lazarus provides a code editor with syntax-highlighting, a visual form designer, and the Lazarus Component Library (LCL). Lazarus is very similar to Delphi, making it ideal for Delphi programmers to utilize. Because the LCL is highly compatible with Delphi's VCL, existing Delphi projects can be easily converted to Lazarus projects.

Lazarus is cross-platform and runs on many platforms, including Linux, BSD, and Mac OS X. Lazarus applications can be created on one platform and compiled on other supporting platforms, making it suitable for many programming tasks. Besides graphical user interface and console applications, Lazarus can also support web-based applications, Android, and iOS applications.

What this book covers

Chapter 1, Installing and Configuring the Lazarus Development Environment, explains the installation and configuration of the Lazarus environment on various platforms, such as Windows, Linux, and FreeBSD.

Chapter 2, Getting to Know the Lazarus IDE – a Quick Tour, is an overview of the basics of the Lazarus IDE, such as the code editor, object inspector, and the LCL palette.

Chapter 3, Creating a Hello World Program, provides an overview of the basics of creating a GUI and console application with Lazarus using the traditional Hello World program and expanding on it.

Chapter 4, Converting Delphi, covers converting an existing Delphi project to a Lazarus project using the Delphi conversion wizard, as well as manually converting the project.

Chapter 5, Creating a Lazarus Component, covers the creation of a custom component that can be added to the component palette to be used in a GUI application.

Chapter 6, The Lazarus Documentation Editor, shows the use of LazDE, the tool for documenting a Lazarus source code unit.

Chapter 7, Rebuilding Lazarus with a GTK2 Interface, covers the rebuilding of the Lazarus interface, using one of the many supported widget sets of Lazarus.

What you need for this book

You will need to use one of the supported OS platforms, such as Windows or Linux, and the Lazarus version for that platform. Some of the source code used is available for download where indicated.

Who this book is for

This book is designed for anyone who has used Delphi in the past. It should also be useful for anyone with a basic programming experience that needs a quick overview of using Lazarus.

Conventions

In this book, you will find a number of styles of text that distinguish between different kinds of information. Here are some examples of these styles and an explanation of their meaning.

Code words in text are shown as follows: "For 32-bit Debian-based distributions, choose the `Lazarus Linux i386 DEB` subfolder."

A block of code is set as follows:

```
program Project1;
{$mode objfpc}{$H+}
uses
  {$IFDEF UNIX}{$IFDEF UseCThreads}
  cthreads,
  {$ENDIF}{$ENDIF}
  Classes, SysUtils, CustApp
  { you can add units after this };
```

Any command-line input or output is written as follows:

```
# gpg -keyserver hkp://pgp.mit.edu:11371 -recv-keys 6A11800F
# gpg -a -export 6A11800F | apt-key add -
```

New terms and **important words** are shown in bold. Words that you see on the screen, in menus or dialog boxes for example, appear in the text like this: "Unless you have a need to change the defaults, just click **Next** through the installation wizard's dialogs."

> Warnings or important notes appear in a box like this.

> Tips and tricks appear like this.

Reader feedback

Feedback from our readers is always welcome. Let us know what you think about this book—what you liked or may have disliked. Reader feedback is important for us to develop titles that you really get the most out of.

To send us general feedback, simply send an e-mail to feedback@packtpub.com, and mention the book title via the subject of your message.

If there is a topic that you have expertise in and you are interested in either writing or contributing to a book, see our author guide on www.packtpub.com/authors.

Customer support

Now that you are the proud owner of a Packt book, we have a number of things to help you get the most from your purchase.

Downloading the example code

You can download the example code files for all Packt books you have purchased from your account at http://www.packtpub.com. If you purchased this book elsewhere, you can visit http://www.packtpub.com/support and register to have the files e-mailed directly to you.

Errata

Although we have taken every care to ensure the accuracy of our content, mistakes do happen. If you find a mistake in one of our books—maybe a mistake in the text or the code—we would be grateful if you would report this to us. By doing so, you can save other readers from frustration and help us improve subsequent versions of this book. If you find any errata, please report them by visiting http://www.packtpub.com/submit-errata, selecting your book, clicking on the **errata submission form** link, and entering the details of your errata. Once your errata are verified, your submission will be accepted and the errata will be uploaded on our website, or added to any list of existing errata, under the Errata section of that title. Any existing errata can be viewed by selecting your title from http://www.packtpub.com/support.

Piracy

Piracy of copyright material on the Internet is an ongoing problem across all media. At Packt, we take the protection of our copyright and licenses very seriously. If you come across any illegal copies of our works, in any form, on the Internet, please provide us with the location address or website name immediately so that we can pursue a remedy.

Please contact us at copyright@packtpub.com with a link to the suspected pirated material.

We appreciate your help in protecting our authors, and our ability to bring you valuable content.

Questions

You can contact us at questions@packtpub.com if you are having a problem with any aspect of the book, and we will do our best to address it.

1
Installing and Configuring the Lazarus Development Environment

In this chapter, we will begin learning about the Lazarus IDE for Free Pascal by installing and configuring Lazarus. We will learn the following:

- Why use Lazarus
- How to install Lazarus on a Linux platform
- How to install Lazarus on a Windows platform
- How to install Lazarus on Mac OS
- How to install Lazarus on FreeBSD
- How to create a basic configuration for Lazarus

Why Lazarus?

Lazarus is an open source, cross-platform integrated development environment (IDE) for the open source Pascal compiler, **Free Pascal (FPC)**. For the purpose of this book, it is to be assumed that when we say Lazarus, we are talking about Lazarus in conjunction with Free Pascal. Free Pascal offers a high degree of compatibility with Delphi's Object Pascal language, which includes many of the same libraries. The **Lazarus Component Library (LCL)** is, in many cases, equivalent to Delphi's VCL, including versions of many of the same controls used to create applications that have a graphical user interface. Just as with Delphi, Lazarus can also be used to create console applications, dynamic link libraries, or web applications.

With all the given similarities to Delphi, it is quite obvious that Lazarus along with Free Pascal can make a suitable open source replacement for Delphi. But, Lazarus is not limited to this. Lazarus can be used to develop Free Pascal applications that can be compiled and run on Linux-based smartphones. It is also possible to develop web applications with Lazarus using additional packages, such as Fpweb, FreeSpider, and Raudus. Compiled libraries can be created, which can be accessed by other programming languages, such as Python or C++.

Lazarus' greatest advantage is that it allows programmers to create cross-platform applications. Lazarus' technique for creating cross-platform applications is referred to as *write once compile anywhere*. This alludes to the fact that you can write applications on one platform, such as Linux, and compile it on different platforms, such as Apple's OS X or Microsoft's Windows operating systems. Currently, Lazarus supports Windows, WinCE, Mac OS X, iOS, Linux, and Android operating systems. In this book, we will focus on Linux and Windows as these are the largest current user bases in the Lazarus community.

Installing Lazarus in Linux

The Lazarus IDE is available as binary packages for Linux in the **Red Hat Package Management (RPM)** format, **Debian (DEB)** format, or in tar gzip format. These packages are available for 32-bit or 64-bit distributions of Linux. Certain distributions of Linux, such as Ubuntu, make Lazarus available through their custom package managers. For information on installing Lazarus using such package management software, check the instructions available from the distribution's website or manuals.

Downloading and installing the Lazarus Linux RPM package

The Lazarus binary RPM package is available from the Lazarus SourceForge.net (`http://sourceforge.net/projects/lazarus/files/`) download area. Once you have accessed this page, choose the correct link for your platform package, in this case either `Lazarus Linux x86_64 RPM` for 64-bit platforms or `Lazarus Linux i386 RPM` for 32-bit platforms. We will be using the 32-bit package for this example. After clicking on the correct link, choose the current release link, in this case `Lazarus 1.0.2`. Once you are in this area, all the packages needed to install Lazarus are available to be downloaded. Download the following packages:

- `Lazarus-1.0.2-1.i386.rpm`
- `fpc-src-2.6.0-0.laz.i686.rpm`
- `fpc-2.6.0-0.laz.i686.rpm`

Also available is the optional package, `fpc-debuginfo-2.6.0-0.laz.i686.rpm`, which provides debug information for the system units. This is only needed if you want to do development for Free Pascal itself, which is beyond the scope of this book.

Requirements

Before installing Free Pascal and Lazarus, the following programs are required on the Linux system:

- GNU as the GNU assembler
- GNU ld or the GNU linker

GNU Make, this is optional but recommended for easy recompiling of the FPC compiler and **Run-Time Library (RTL)**.

Lazarus requires the following libraries:

GTK+ 2.x or Qt: Most Linux distributions already install GTK+ 2.x. You can also download the libraries from `http://www.gtk.org`. Qt is also supported by most distributions and is installed together with KDE.

To begin the installation of Lazarus, log into your system as a root user. First install the Free Pascal for the Lazarus package with the following command:

```
# rpm -UvH fpc-2.6.0-0.laz.i686.rpm
```

After the successful completion of this package, next we will need to install the Free Pascal source code package. The Free Pascal source code package is required to operate certain functions in Lazarus. If the IDE cannot find the Free Pascal source, the user will be presented with a warning box with the following message:

The Free Pascal source was not found. Some functions will not work.

To install the Free Pascal source, use the following command:

```
# rpm -UvH fpc-src-2.6.0-0.laz.i686.rpm
```

After the successful completion of the installation of the Free Pascal source, all that is left to do is to install the Lazarus IDE itself with the following command:

```
# rpm -UvH Lazarus-1.0-1.i386.rpm
```

With the successful completion of these three packages, you are ready to use the Lazarus IDE. Under the GNOME desktop, Lazarus can be accessed from the **Applications** menu under the **Programming** submenu.

Downloading and installing the Lazarus Linux DEB package

For Debian-based Linux distributions, the SourceForge.net Lazarus repository contains Debian packages for 32-bit and 64-bit distributions. Access the SourceForge.net repository at `http://sourceforge.net/projects/lazarus/files/`. For 32-bit Debian-based distributions, choose the `Lazarus Linux i386 DEB` subfolder. For 64-bit Debian-based distributions, choose the `Lazarus Linux amd64 DEB` subfolder. Next, choose the current Lazarus release, which at the time of writing is `Lazarus 1.0.2`. Download all the Debian packages within this folder.

For 32-bit systems:

* `lazarus_1.0.2-0_i386.deb`
* `fpc-src_2.6.0-120824_i386.deb`
* `fpc_2.6.0-120824_i386.deb`

For 64-bit systems:

* `lazarus_1.0.2-0_amd64.deb`
* `fpc-src_2.6.0-120824_amd64.deb`
* `fpc_2.6.0-120824_amd64.deb`

Once the packages are downloaded, install them using the following command:

```
dpkg -i <package_name>
```

Install each of the packages for Free Pascal, Free Pascal Source, and the Lazarus IDE.

Lazarus for Ubuntu

There is an Ubuntu repository available at `http://www.hu.freepascal.org` that contains Lazarus and FPC debs. This repository can be used with `apt-get`. Before using this repository with `apt-get`, it first needs to be added to the apt.

First, we need to add the repository's gpg key to the apt keys with the following commands as a root user:

```
# gpg -keyserver hkp://pgp.mit.edu:11371 -recv-keys 6A11800F
# gpg -a -export 6A11800F | apt-key add -
```

Next, add the repository by editing /etc/apt/sources.list, adding the following line:

```
deb http://www.hu.freepascal.org/lazarus/lazarus-stable universe
```

Once the repository is added to the list of available repositories, Lazarus can be installed with the following commands, again as root:

```
# apt-get update
# apt-get install lazarus
```

Installing under Windows

The Lazarus and Free Pascal binary packages for the Windows operating systems are available from the SourceForge.net repository at http://sourceforge.net/projects/lazarus/files/. The Windows installer packages include both Free Pascal and Lazarus in an easy-to-install package. Choose either the Lazarus Windows 32 bits or Lazarus Widows 64 bits subfolder depending on your OS version. Next choose the current version of the Lazarus subfolder, which at the time of writing is Lazarus 1.02. Click on the lazarus-1.0.2-fpc-2.6.0-win32.exe Windows installer package. For Windows 32-bit operating systems or for Windows 64-bit operating systems, click on lazarus-1.0.2-fpc-2.6.0-win64.exe.

If you intend to develop applications for WinCE using Lazarus, you will need to download the WinCE installer package, that is, lazarus-1.0.2-fpc-2.6.0-cross-arm-wince-win32.exe. There is no 64-bit version available.

Once you have the files downloaded, double-click on the executable file to start the installation process. The installation process, as with most Windows installers, is straightforward. Unless you have a need to change the defaults, just click **Next** through the installation wizard's dialogs. One dialog to note is the **Select Components** dialog (shown in the following screenshot), this dialog defaults to having all applicable file extensions, such as .pas, opened with the Lazarus IDE. If you also have Delphi installed, you may want to consider changing these options.

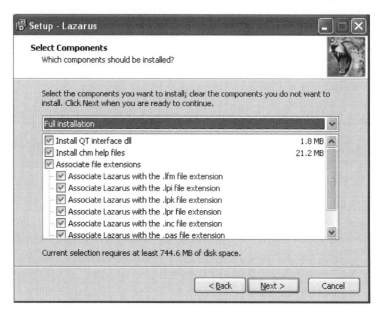

Installing under other OSes such as FreeBSD or Mac OS X

Although Lazarus is targeted mainly for Linux and Windows operating systems, there are also binary packages available for Mac OS X. FreeBSD makes Free Pascal and Lazarus available through its ports collections. It is also possible to run Lazarus on other operating systems, such as Haiku, by compiling Lazarus and Free Pascal from source.

Installing Lazarus on Mac OS X

Lazarus and Free Pascal are available as disk images (`.dmg` files) for Mac OS X for Intel-based Macs and PowerPC-based Macs from the SourceForge.net Repository at `http://sourceforge.net/projects/lazarus/files/`. The Mac OS X versions of Lazarus require the installation of Apple Developer Tools. This can be installed from the Mac OS X installation disks or downloaded from the **Apple Developers Connection (ADC)** at `http://developer.apple.com`. ADC requires registration, which is free. Once these tools have been installed, go to the SourceForge.net repository and select the correct subfolder for your Mac, Lazarus Mac OS X PowerPC, or Lazarus Mac OS X i386. Then choose the latest release of the Lazarus subfolder, which is `Lazarus 1.0.2` at the time of writing, and download the disk images. For Mac OS X PowerPC, download the following:

- `fpcsrc-2.6.0.powerpc-macosx.dmg`
- `fpc-2.6.0.powerpc-macosx.dmg`
- `lazarus-1.0.2-powerpc-macosx.dmg`

For Mac OS X Intel:

- `fpcsrc-2.6.0.powerpc-macosx.dmg`
- `fpc-2.6.0.powerpc-macosx.dmg`
- `lazarus-1.0.2-20121009-i386-macosx.dmg`

Once the disk image files are downloaded, install them in the following order:

- `fpc`: The Free Pascal compiler
- `fpcsrc`: The Free Pascal compiler source
- `lazarus`: The Lazarus IDE

After installation, the Lazarus application can be found in `/Developer/lazarus`, the Free Pascal source files are in `/usr/local/share/fpcsrc`.

Installing under FreeBSD

The FreeBSD ports collection contains, at the time of writing, 91 separate ports for Free Pascal. These ports are divided into subcategories such as `graphics`, `math`, and `multimedia`. This is in keeping with the FreeBSD philosophy of only installing necessary packages to keep this system as small as possible and easily maintainable. For Lazarus, the ports collection contains six separate ports; among them are GTK+, GTK2+, and Qt toolkit versions of Lazarus. The simplest way to install Free Pascal is to log in as a root user and issue the following commands:

```
# cd /usr/ports/lang/fpc
# make install clean
```

This will install the Free Pascal meta port. **Meta port** in FreeBSD is a port that installs multiple sub ports. In this case, the `fpc` meta port will install all 91 Free Pascal port. In addition to these ports, any requirements not installed on the system will also be automatically installed. If you are an advanced FreeBSD user and know exactly the type of development you are going to do with Lazarus and Free Pascal, you can install only the needed individual ports of the 91 available.

The easiest way to install Lazarus is to use the meta port located in `/usr/ports/editors/lazarus`. Remain logged in as root and issue the following commands:

```
# cd /usr/ports/editors/lazarus
# make config
```

This will bring up the **Options for Lazarus** dialog box as seen in the screenshot that follows. In this dialog, you can choose to either install the **GTK2** interface or the **QT4** interface for the IDE. You can only choose one of the two options, choosing both will cause an error during installation.

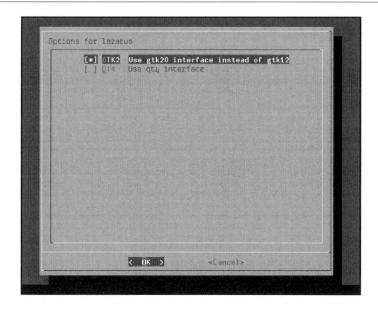

After selecting the desired interface and selecting **OK**, continue installing by issuing the following command:

```
# make install clean
```

Once the installation is complete, Lazarus will be installed in /usr/local/bin and can be started with the following command:

```
$ /usr/local/bin/startlazarus
```

For operating systems that don't have a binary package available, Lazarus can be built using the source code.

Installing from source

Lazarus and Free Pascal source code is available through **Subversion (SVN)**. The SVN repositories provide the most up-to-date source code available. The SVN repositories also allow you to track only the changes in the source. Although, SVN access requires an Internet connection, it does not require the user to be root.

When downloading the source, you need to make sure that you have enough free space. The initial checkout requires approximately 270 MB of free space. To begin the installation from source, first make sure that current working folder is the folder that you want the source code to be present in. For the initial checkout, use the following command:

```
$ svn checkout http://svn.freepascal.org/svn/lazarus/trunk/ lazarus
```

This will download the latest available source code to the `lazarus` subfolder, which will be created in the current folder. Once the download is completed, compile the source code by using the following command:

```
$ cd lazarus
$ make
```

Once the build is complete, Lazarus can be started from the current folder with the following command:

```
$ ./startlazarus
```

To keep Lazarus up-to-date, from the parent folder of the Lazarus source code, use the following commands:

```
$ svn update lazarus
$ cd lazarus
$ make clean all
```

This will rebuild the Lazarus IDE without packages. After the build is done, then use the following command to link to the existing Lazarus packages:

```
$ ./lazbuild –build-ide=
```

If you are building from source on a BSD-based system, you will need to use gmake instead of make.

On the Windows platform, if you have Delphi installed, you must modify your PATH variable or delete the Delphi version of make.

Configuring the Lazarus development environment

After a successful installation of Lazarus and Free Pascal, it may be necessary to set up a few environmental settings so Lazarus can function correctly. Start Lazarus on the initial start up. You may see the informational error notifying that Lazarus cannot find the Free Pascal source directory. To correct this, open the Lazarus **IDE Options** dialog which looks like the screenshot that follows. The **IDE Options** dialog is accessed under the **Environment** menu and the **Options** submenu.

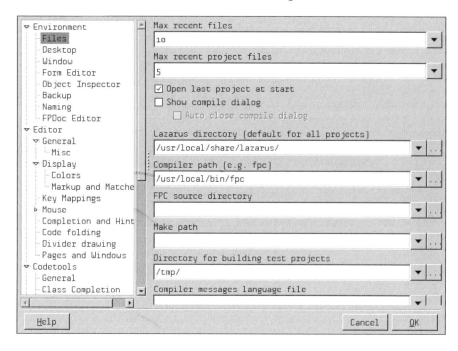

When you initially access this dialog, you can see that the **FPC source directory** textbox is empty, click the ellipse button and enter the source directory path.

For Linux/BSD, enter the following:

```
/usr/local/src/FPC
```

For Windows, the **IDE Options** menu is located under the **Tools** menu. The default Free Pascal source folder is `c:\lazarus\fpc\2.6.0\source`.

If you did not install Lazarus using the defaults, choose the folder in which you installed Lazarus.

Another import option that is not set in the Linux version is the debugger. To access the debugger settings, scroll down in the left window of the **Options** menu and select **Debugger**. In the right window pane, select the drop-down box with the heading **Debugger type and path**. Select the **GNU Debugger (gdb)** option. Once selected, the path should populate itself.

Summary

In this chapter we learned that Lazarus is an open source integrated development environment for the Free Pascal language that is similar to Delphi. Lazarus contains the LCL, which is its version of Delphi's VCL. Lazarus can be used to create console as well as GUI applications. Because of its similarities to Delphi, it can be used as a replacement for Delphi.

Lazarus can be installed on Linux platforms either by using the package management tool of the specific Linux distribution or by installing it from the binary or source files located on the SourceForge.net repository.

Lazarus can also be installed on the Windows platforms, either 32-bit, or 64-bit using the packages available on the SourceForge.net repository.

There are also .dmg package files available at SourceForge.net for installing Lazarus on Mac OS.

The FreeBSD project makes Lazarus available through its ports system. There are 91 separate packages related to Lazarus and Free Pascal. There is also a meta package that will install all the separate packages or a subset thereof.

We learned how to set up the IDE options for the FPC source folder and the GNU debugger.

With the successful installation and updating of the settings, we now have a basic Lazarus development environment. We are ready to take on programming with Free Pascal and Lazarus, but first let's take some time to familiarize ourselves with the Lazarus IDE.

2
Getting to Know the Lazarus IDE – a Quick Tour

In this chapter we are going to examine the Lazarus interface. We will cover the following topics:

- Learn about the different parts of the default interface layout, such as:
  - The **Source Editor** window
  - The **Object Inspector** window
  - The **Component Tree** window

- Learn about **Main Menu**
- Learn about **LCL Palette**

For a Delphi programmer, the Lazarus IDE should look quite familiar. The default layout of Lazarus is extremely similar to Delphi's default layout, as you can see in the following screenshot. **LCL Component Palette** is located on the topmost window, along with the main menu and quick access icons. To the left is the **Object Inspector** window. The **Object Inspector** window also contains the **Component Tree** window, which displays a tree view of all the components used on the current active form of the project, by default **Form1**. Next to the **Object Inspector** window is the **Source Editor** window, which contains a tab for each individual source code file of the project. Finally, below the **Source Editor** window is the **Message** window, which displays import information, such as build warnings and errors. Let's look at these windows in more detail.

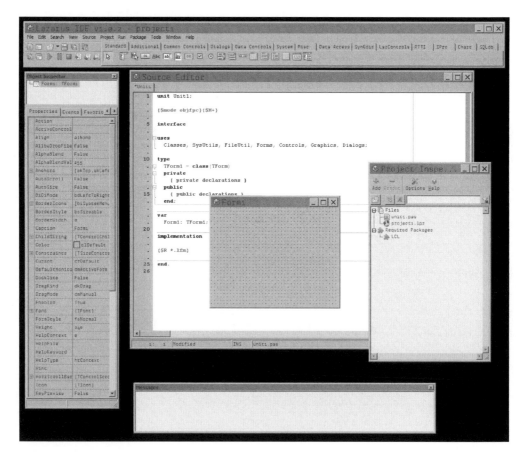

The Object Inspector window

The first tab of the **Object Inspector** window is the **Properties** tab. The **Properties** tab contains the published properties of the graphical component elements contained in a form, such as Name, Position, and Visible. Clicking on a component on the form or selecting it in the **Component Tree** window makes its properties accessible in the **Properties** tab. Right-clicking on the **Properties** tab displays a pop-up menu with the **Show Hints**, **Show Components Tree**, and **Options** entries.

When the developer places his mouse cursor over the property of the active component, such as **Align**, having **Show Hints** enabled will display a pop-up message with help concerning that property. The **Options** entry opens the **IDE Options** dialog, displaying the **Environment** options tree with the **Object Inspector** branch selected. Primarily, these options are just for setting the look of the **Object Inspector** branch with options for setting colors or showing or not showing certain elements of the **Object Inspector** branch. One very useful option is the **Show information** box. Checking this will display an additional box at the bottom of the **Object Inspector** window that will show more information about properties, including a more detailed description of what the property does, what package the component is contained in, and reference to related properties if available.

The second tab in the **Object Inspector** window is the **Events** tab, which allows the developer to bind a procedure to a component's event. Double-clicking on the right column, for any event, will create a procedure stub in the unit's source file. A unit is composed of a pascal source file (`.pas`) and a form file (`.lfm`). For example, say we have a project that contains a form called `Form1` and that form contains a button named `Button1`, and it is the current active component in the **Object Inspector** window. Click on the **Events** tab; double-clicking in the right column of the **OnClick** event should produce the following procedure stub:

```
procedure TForm1.Button1Click(Sender: TObject);
begin
end;
```

Complete the procedure's code and you now have a button that runs a procedure when clicked.

Downloading the example code

You can download the example code files for all Packt books you have purchased from your account at http://www.packtpub.com . If you purchased this book elsewhere, you can visit http://www.packtpub.com/support and register to have the files e-mailed directly to you.

Next is the **Favorites** tab. This tab contains the most used, or favorite, properties and events of a component. Different components will have a varying number of default entries on the **Favorites** tab. You can add your own favorites by selecting either a property name on the **Properties** tab and/or an event's name on the **Events** tab; then right-click on it. A pop-up menu should appear; select **Add To Favorites** and the element is added to the favorites for this component.

The last tab is the **Restricted** tab. This tab gives you access to properties that are not usable on certain graphical widget sets, such as **GTK**, **Qt**, or the native interfaces of Windows or Mac OS X. Next to each property name you will see one or more icons that represent the widget set that the property will have no effect on.

As mentioned in the preceding section, right-clicking on a property name or event name will access a pop-up menu. This menu includes the same entries that are on the pop-up menu that is accessed by clicking on the tab name as well as a number of useful additional entries. The entry **Set to default** will, as implied, reset the value of the property to its default. The **Jump to declaration** entry will open the source code unit that contains this component and highlight the declaration of the property being hovered over.

The Component Tree window

The **Component Tree** window is located in the top window of the **Object Tree** dialog and can be made visible or hidden by checking or unchecking the **Show Component Tree** entry on any of the pop-up menus that are accessed by right-clicking on the **Object Inspector** dialog. The components of the application are shown in a parent-child relationship on a tree diagram. Right-clicking on the window gives you access to a pop-up menu that allows you to copy, cut, paste, and delete the selected component. Copying will create a new component when pasted. You can cut and paste a component into and out of different container type components such as **TPanel**. There is also a menu entry titled **Z-order** that allows you to adjust what layer of the form the component is anchored to. This is only effective for container components, such as **TPanel**.

The Source Editor window

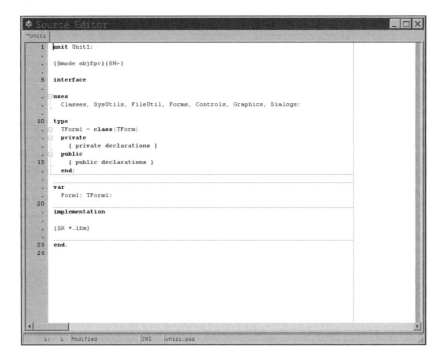

The **Source Editor** window contains a tab for each opened unit's source code. The **Source Editor** features include code highlighting, code completion, and refactoring. The **Source Editor** options can be accessed by right-clicking on the window and selecting the **Options** entry in the pop-up menu. Options such as code folding, code color highlighting, and the delay of displaying the code hints and completion boxes are displayed. The pop-up menu also contains entries to change file settings, such as displaying the code line numbers, and code highlighting colors, and debug settings, such as toggling of breakpoints, evaluation, and modification of expressions. We will cover many of these options in more detail in *Chapter 3, Creating a Hello World Program*.

Main menu, quick icons, and the LCL Palette window

The main menu, quick icons, and the LCL Palette window are at the top-most part of the Lazarus IDE window. Quick icons is the Lazarus terminology for the icons located to the left of the LCL palette. Unlike Delphi, these icons cannot be modified in position or visibility. The icons are shortcuts to the more commonly used entries in the main menu, such as **Run**, **Save**, **View From**, or **Create new unit**. The main menu entries should be very familiar to users of Delphi or most integrated development environments. That being said, let's explore some of the more important main menu entries.

Project Options

The **Projects Options** dialog can be accessed through the toolbar under the **Project** entry or by using the keyboard shortcut *Ctrl + Shift + F11*. The **Project Options** dialog allows you to set such application settings as the **Title** and **Icon** of the application. Under the **Forms** entry in the left-side window, you can choose which forms to include and exclude from the building of the project. The **Version Info** option lets you set the version of the executable file that is compiled. Checking the **Automatically increment build number** checkbox is particularly useful. Checking it will cause the build number to increase on a successful build, making it easier for you to keep a track of builds. You can also set information such as copyright, product name, and company name of the executable.

Compiler Options are also available through the **Project Options** dialog. The widget type can be set under the **Build Modes** node. This is done by selecting a value for **Macro name** and **LCLWidgetType** and setting the **Macro value** to one of the available values. The default setting for the widget type is GTK2 on Linux. The developer can change this to any of the usable widget types such as Qt or Win32; changing this can help in cross-platform compatibility of your application. Under the **Parsing** option, you can change the Pascal syntax, and the parser will interpret the code as Object Pascal, Free Pascal, or Delphi.

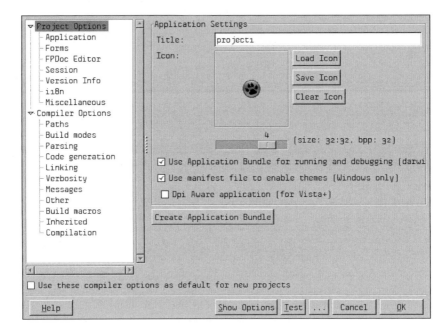

The **Code Generation** option allows you to change the compiling options for **Target Platform** and **Optimizations**. **Target Platform** can be changed to any supported platform of the Free Pascal compiler, such as Linux, FreeBSD, Darwin, Win32, and so on. **Target CPU** and **Target processor** can also be adjusted, but take care in doing so as you don't want to select an invalid combination, such as a power CPU with Pentium processor. There are four different levels of optimization (level 0-3) that can be applied to compiling; normally, level 1 (the default) should be used. When building a project for release, you may want to consider using level 2 or 3. Other options allow you to control what warnings and informational messages are displayed in the **Message** window when compiling your project, or call certain commands before compiling or running the project. Once you have set your options, you can make these settings the default for all projects by checking the **Use these compiler options as the default for new projects** box located on the bottom-left of the dialog. The **Show Options** button will show the developer the command-line options of FPC. The **Test** button will check the compiler options and display any warnings or errors.

The Run menu

The **Run** menu can be accessed by clicking **Run** on the toolbar. The **Run** menu contains options for building, debugging, and running an application. The three options for building a project are **Build**, **Build all**, and **Quick compile**. The **Build** option is the default building method and can also be accessed with the keyboard shortcut *Ctrl + F9*; it only builds units files that have changed since the last build. The **Build all** option will build all project files irrespective of whether they have changed or not since the last build. The **Quick compile** option will compile the units quickly by omitting the assembly and linking stages of building.

The **Run** command, which can also be accessed by clicking on *F9*, will run the project. If the project has units that have changed and have not been built yet, they will be built first. The program will run until either a breakpoint is reached, the program encounters an error, or the developer exits or stops the program.

The Tools menu

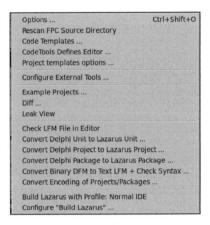

The **Tools** menu gives the developer a number of predefined utilities and the ability and access to external tools. There are utilities to convert Delphi projects, packages, and units to their Lazarus equivalents. These utilities will be discussed in more depth in *Chapter 4, Converting a Delphi Project*. The **Code Templates** entry opens a dialog that allows the developer to view and edit or create his own code templates. A code template is a collection of code snippets or expression stubs that are assigned to an abbreviation that allows it to be inserted into the source code using the *Ctrl + J* keyboard shortcut.

Let's see an example. In the Source Editor, type `arrayc` and then press *Ctrl + J*. You should now see the abbreviation expanded to the following:

```
array[0..1] of Type = ();
```

The **Configure External Tools** entry allows the developer to add an external application or commands to a keyboard shortcut within the IDE that can perform some action on the current file(s) or project. Once you have successfully added a new external tool, its entry will be displayed under the **Configure External Tools** entry.

The **Diff** entry compares two of the opened units in the **Source Editor** window for a project against each other for differences in the code. The opened units' names will be displayed in a drop-down box. If you want to compare units that are not opened or files that are not part of the project, you can select them using the ellipse button next to the **Filename** drop-down box.

The **Example Projects** entry allows the developer access to a number of example Lazarus projects. The **Example Project** dialog will show a listing of all the available projects. When selected, a brief description of what the program demonstrates is displayed, if it is available.

The last two entries on the **Tools** menu are something unique to the Lazarus IDE, **Build Lazarus with Profile: Normal IDE** and **Configure "Build Lazarus"**. These two options allow the developer to rebuild and configure the rebuilding of the Lazarus IDE itself. Settings can be optimized for the widget type, operating system, and CPU. We will look at rebuilding the Lazarus IDE in *Chapter 7, Rebuilding Lazarus with GTK2 Interface*.

The LCL Palette

The LCL Palette is the heart of the Lazarus IDE, as it contains both visible and non-visible components that can be used to create a Free Pascal based application. Visible components are components such as a button or a textbox, that can be seen on a GUI application. Non-visible components have nothing that can be viewed in a GUI, such as a database connection component or a timer. The developer adds the component to a **TForm** by selecting the desired component and then either double-clicking on it or clicking on the form. Let's look at some of the individual tabs and components of the LCL Palette.

The Standard tab

The **Standard** tab is the first LCL Palette and contains the most used form controls; the components include:

- TMainMenu: It is the first component of the **Standard** tab. When initially added to the form, nothing is visible. The developer must add items to the menu using either the **Object Inspector** and the **Items** property or right-clicking on the component and selecting **Menu Editor**. Once the developer has added some items, they will become visible on the form as the main menu text.

- TPopupMenu: It is an invisible component, since it creates nothing when added to the form. It needs menu information just like TMainMenu; but, unlike TMainMenu, nothing will be displayed until runtime and, even then, only when the pop-up menu is called in the code.

- TToggleBox: It is a button that stays in the pressed or unpressed state after clicking, depending on its starting state, unlike TButton, which always returns to the unpressed state.

- TGroupBox: It is a container component that holds other components and can be used to group components, such as radio buttons, together physically.

- TFrame: It is a container component that is descended from TForm; but, unlike a TFrom component, a TFrame component can be embedded in a TForm component or another TFrame component. This ability allows you to use the same Tform component on multiple forms so the same controls and layout can be reused without all the extra work.

The Additional tab

The following components are descendants of a control on the **Standard** tab:

- TBitButton: It is a button that can have a small image embedded on it.

- TSpeedButton: It is a button that never changes state or gets focus, but, when clicked, it will start a process.

- TNoteBook: It is a container control that holds pages. These pages are other container controls and the notebook will never contain tabs.

- TStringGrid: It is a container for displaying text information in column-and-row format, similar to a spreadsheet in appearance.

The Common Control tab

The **Common Control** tab contains control components that are used often in GUI applications, which are as follows:

- TTreeView: It is a control that displays list information in a hierarchical layout. The list items can be displayed as just text and can also contain an image.

- TPageControl: It is a control that displays a tab on the edge of a multipage component.

- TImageList: It is an invisible control that contains a list of images, from files, that can be accessed by other components, such as TBitButton or TTreeView.

The Dialogs tab

The **Dialogs** tab contains dialogs commonly used in GUI applications. These components are invisible and need to be triggered programmatically, usually from the **OnClick** event of a button.

- `TOpenDialog`: It shows the **File Open** dialog and allows the selection of the file that is opened. The `Execute` method should be called to show the dialog itself, as in the following code:

```
procedure TForm1.Button1Click(Sender: TObject);
begin
    OpenDialog1.Execute;
end;
```

- `TSaveDialog`: It shows the file saving dialog and allows the saving of a file. As with `TOpenDialog`, showing the dialog must be done programmatically.

- `TPrintDialog`: It is a dialog for choosing which printer to print to.

- `TReplaceDialog`: It is a dialog for finding and replacing text.

The Data Controls tab

The **Data Controls** tab contains controls that are data-aware. Meaning, these controls can be linked to a database through data source and don't require additional programming to be populated with data from the database. Most of these controls are recognizable, as they are versions of controls on either the **Standard** or the **Additional** tabs.

- `TDBNavigator`: It is a navigation bar that allows moving through the records in a data set.

The SQLdb tab

The **SQLdb** tab contains controls for connecting to different databases such as MySQL, PostgreSQL, Oracle, MS SQL, or SQLite. These controls can be used with the data controls through a `TDatasource`.

- `TSQLQuery`: It is a control that represents a dataset result from a SQL query. The control can also be used to modify data in a database by use of an insert, update or delete query.

- `TSQLTransaction`: This component encapsulates the transaction on a database. The different database connectors in the **SQLdb** tab require `TSQLTransaction` for managing query transactions.

There are a number of different components for connecting to databases on the **SQLdb** tab; among them are:

- `TODBCConnection`: It connects to a database using ODBC.

- `TOracleConnection`: It connects to an Oracle database.

- `TSQLite3Connection`: It connects to a SQLite database.

- `TMySQL50Connection`: It connects to a MySQL database.

Summary

In this chapter we learned about the different parts of Lazarus. The **Main Menu** area located in the top-most window, by default, contains various submenus, such as the **Run** menu, which contains entries for compiling, running, and debugging an application, and the **Project** menu, from which new projects can be created. Options such as the application title and icon can be set using the **Projects Options** entry.

The **Source Editor** window includes features such as code highlighting, code completion, refactoring, and code folding.

The **Object Inspector** window allows access to the published properties and events of a graphical component that has been added to a form.

The **Component Tree** window, which is located in the top window of the **Object Inspector** window, shows the components of a form in a parent-child relationship. Components can be added or edited using **Component Tree**.

Finally, we learned about the **LCL Palette**, which has multiple tabs, such as **SQLdb**, **Common Controls**, and **Misc,** that contain various components that can be used in applications.

Now that we have briefly looked over the IDE, we can begin creating applications using Lazarus. We'll do this by creating the traditional Hello World project.

3
Creating a Hello World Program

After having installed Lazarus and becoming familiar with the **integrated development environment (IDE)**, a good starting point is the traditional Hello World program. In this chapter, we will:

- First build a console application for the traditional Hello World program, followed by a GUI version of Hello World

- Expand upon the GUI version to begin learning to use the debugger features of the IDE

- Finally, we will look at deploying an application created in Lazarus

Hello World console application version

When Lazarus is started, it will either show the last opened project or start with a new GUI application. Select **New Project**. When the **New Project** dialog appears, select **Console application**. Click on the **OK** button. The **New console application** dialog is now visible. First, rename the application to THelloConsoleApplication from default **TMyApplication** in the **Application class name** textbox. Next, change default **Title** from My Application to Hello World. Leave all the rest of the settings to default. Now, the **New console application** dialog should look like the following screenshot (leave the rest of the defaults as they are, and click on the **OK** button):

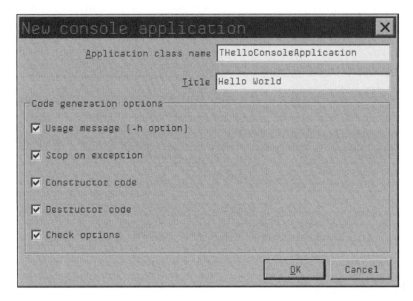

The **Source Editor** window will appear with the auto-generated code for a console application. Let's examine some of the auto-generated code before we go any further.

This first section of the auto-generated code shows the program directive. Here, it is Project1; since the project has not been saved yet, this is the default name. When the project is saved, it can be changed. Save the project now and accept the defaults. The next line starts with a compiler directive to set the mode of the compiler, {$mode objfpc}, which is Object Pascal and Free Pascal. This is followed by the compiler directive, {$H+}, which sets the compiler to treat the keyword string as AnsiString. The compiler default setting is to treat the string as not an AnsiStrings type or {$H-}. Note that if the directive {$mode delphi} is given, strings will be treated as AnsiStrings.

The next section of the code is the uses clause. The uses clause lists units, separated by a comma, that are used by this unit. The first line in this unit clause contains two conditional compilation directives. Conditional compilation directives start with the {$IFDEF name} directive and end with the {$ENDIF} directives. With conditional compilation directives, if the symbol name in the statement is defined, then the compiler will continue and use the contained and enclosed directive. Otherwise, the directive is passed over. In this case, if the names UNIX and UseCThreads are defined, the unit cthreads will be used; otherwise, it is not used. The next line of code lists three units that will be used in this unit, Classes, SysUtils, and CustApp, followed by a comment and a semicolon (;) that ends the uses clause:

```
program Project1;

{$mode objfpc}{$H+}

uses
  {$IFDEF UNIX}{$IFDEF UseCThreads}
  cthreads,
  {$ENDIF}{$ENDIF}
  Classes, SysUtils, CustApp
  { you can add units after this };
```

The next section of code is the type clause, which defines the class used in this unit. The first line is just a comment naming the class definition to follow. The first line of the class declaration, THelloConsoleApplication = class(TCustomApplication), states that the class THelloConsoleApplication is a descendant from the parent class, TCustomApplication. A descendant class has access to all the functions, procedures, and properties of its parent class that are not declared as private. The first section of the class definition is the protected section. This section contains procedures, functions, and properties that are accessible to any class, which is a descendant of this class. For THelloConsoleApplication, only the definition of the procedure DoRun is contained in the protected section. Notice the keyword override; this lets the compiler know that you intend to re-implement a method of the parent class, and to ignore the implementation that would have been inherited by the descendant. The public section follows and has some important procedure definitions that all classes must have. The constructor keyword defines the procedure that will be called when an object of this class type is created. It is convention that the constructor procedure is called Create, but it could be called anything the developer would like. The constructor for THelloConsoleApplication has a parameter, TheOwner of the type Tcomponent, and it overrides the parent constructor.

The next method is the `destructor` procedure definition. This is the procedure that is called when the class is destroyed. Again, this procedure is an overridden procedure of the parent class. The last line is the definition of the procedure, `WriteHelp`. This definition has the keyword `virtual` after it. The `virtual` keyword allows this procedure to be overridden in a class derived from `THelloConsoleApplication`. The `type` clause can also contain a `private` and `publish` section. Published class members are like `public` members, except they are available at design time and will appear in the **Object Inspector** window.

```
type

  { THelloConsoleApplication }

  THelloConsoleApplication = class(TCustomApplication)
  protected
    procedure DoRun; override;
  public
    constructor Create(TheOwner: TComponent); override;
    destructor Destroy; override;
    procedure WriteHelp; virtual;
  end;
```

The next section of the code is the implementation section. This is where the code for each class procedure and function is written or implemented. The first implemented method is `DoRun`. The first piece of the `DoRun` procedure that follows contains a `var` section in the beginning of the main block of code. The `var` section is where variables that are local to procedure are defined. Variables that are local to a method cannot be accessed outside the method. In this method, `ErrorMsg` is defined as a string:

```
procedure THelloConsoleApplication.DoRun;
var
  ErrorMsg: String;
begin
  // quick check parameters
  ErrorMsg:=CheckOptions('h','help');
  if ErrorMsg<>'' then begin
    ShowException(Exception.Create(ErrorMsg));
    Terminate;
    Exit;
  end;
```

The preceding section of the DoRun procedure checks for command line parameters h or help using the CheckOptions function from the CustApp unit. If either of the options is found, then there is no error, and the variable ErrorMsg is left as an empty string (''). If there is an error when checking, the error message returned from CheckOptions is then assigned to ErrorMsg. If ErrorMsg is not blank, then show an error message to the user, stop the program, and exit. If there is no error, then execution will continue on to the next section of code.

The next section of code is as follows:

```
// parse parameters
if HasOption('h','help') then begin
   WriteHelp;
   Terminate;
   Exit;
 end;

 { add your program here }

 // stop program loop
 Terminate;
end;
```

The preceding section of code checks if either the h or help option was given on the command line using the HasOption function from the CustApp unit. If so, the procedure WriteHelp is called. After WriteHelp has returned control, then the application stops execution and exits. If neither of the parameters was found, then execution would have passed to the statement after the if block, which, in this case, is the Terminate statement.

The implementation of the class constructor is given next. The implementation of this constructor is very basic. The constructor first calls the parent class constructor, passing to it the TheOwner parameter; this is indicated by the keyword inherited. For a constructor, it is a good practice to first call the parent class constructor, although it is not required. If inherited is not followed by a method name, it will call the same method name in the parent class with the same parameters as the calling method. In this class, the statement inherited; would have been sufficient enough. Finally, the property StopOnException is set to true. StopOnException is inherited by THelloConsoleApplication from its parent class TCustomApplication.

```
constructor THelloConsoleApplication.Create(TheOwner: TComponent);
begin
  inherited Create(TheOwner);
  StopOnException:=True;
end;
```

The destructor implementation is quite simple; it just calls the Destroy method of the parent class. The last method in the implementation section is the method we defined in the public type section, WriteHelp. As generated, this method will only write a single help message to the console.

The next section of code can be thought of as the main function of C.

The global variable Application is declared as an instance of THelloConsoleApplication. The object application is then instantiated or created by calling the constructor of THelloConsoleApplication and passing the parameter nil. The paramater nil is a constant for a pointer with no value. In the case of the constructor of THelloConsoleApplication, the object created will have no owner. Next, the **Title** property of THelloConsoleApplication, which was inherited from its parent, is assigned. The class method Run is then executed, and finally, the Free method is called, each inherited from the parent class.

```
var
  Application: THelloConsoleApplication;
begin
  Application:=THelloConsoleApplication.Create(nil);
  Application.Title:='Hello World';
  Application.Run;
  Application.Free;
end.
```

If this program was to be compiled and run in its current state, it would not do much. If it was invoked with -h on the command line, then a short message would be output to the console. If no parameter was given, it would seem that nothing happens when run.

Modifying the code

To make this program more of a traditional Hello World program, it needs to print the phrase to the console. To do so, in the DoRun method under the comment, { add your program here }, insert the following code:

```
Writeln("Hello World!");
```

Save the changes by clicking on the **Save All quick** icon, or use the keyboard shortcut, *Ctrl + Shift + S*. Now, the program is ready to be compiled and run.

Compiling and running

Compile the program through the main menu by going to **Run | Compile**, or use the keyboard shortcut, *Ctrl + F9*. After the build is complete, the message window should display the following message:

```
Project "Hello World" successfully built
```

Since the build was successful, the application can now be built. As this is a console application, we need to run the executable from the command line. If using Linux/Unix, start with xterm. If using Windows, start the command prompt with cmd.exe from **Run** in the **Start** menu on Windows XP, or search programs and files from the **Start** menu in Windows 7. Change to the directory in which the project was saved. To execute the program on Unix/Linux at the command prompt, type the command $ ./project1. On Windows, type C:\Code\Lazarus\project1>project1.

The program will run, and **Hello World** will be printed to the screen.

Run in IDE

From the main menu, select **Run | Run Parameters**, then check the box for **Use launching application**.

Hello World graphical user interface version

Creating a Hello World console application has shown the basics of writing a program using the Lazarus IDE, but to fully explore the power of Lazarus, a graphical user interface application should be built.

Close the current project and start a new project. Just like what was done when creating a new console application project, but this time in the **Create a new project** window, choose **Application**.

A blank form with the title **Form1** will appear along with a unit of auto-generated code. The auto-generated code for a GUI is, quite noticeably, sparse as compared to the auto-generated code for a console application. The uses clause contains the most common and necessary units for creating a GUI application. A few units may not be necessary depending on the function of the application. In the case of the Hello World program, the units **FileUtil** and **Graphics** are not needed. The type clause contains a declaration of TForm1 deriving from TForm, but there are no properties or method declared in the public or private sections. The implementation section is empty except for a compiler directive, {$R *.lfm}.

This directive tells the compiler to include all files with the extension lfm. These are the files that the form information is stored in.

Adding components and modifying code

The GUI version of the Hello World program will have a button that, when clicked by the user, will show a pop-up message saying **Hello World**.

To start, double-click on the **TButton** icon of the **Standard** tab of the component palette. A button with the text Button1 will appear on the form. Looking at the unit in the **Source Editor** window, notice that the unit named StdCtrls has been added to the uses clause and that the declaration of Button1 is added to the class definition.

The Button1 declaration was not placed in the public or private section of the class declaration. In fact, it has no explicit access modifier. Fields or methods in the unlabeled section of the class definition are declared as published.

Double-click on **Button1** on the form. This will create a method `stub` for the click event of `Button1`. To create a pop-up message, use the `MessageDlg` function that is contained in the `Dialogs` unit. `MessageDlg` is an overloaded method, which means that `MessageDlg` can be called with a number of different parameters. Using the simplest version, the completed code should look as follows:

```
procedure TForm1.Button1Click(Sender: TObject);
begin
    MessageDlg('Hello World', TMsgDlgType.mtInformation,[TMsgDlgBtn.
mbOK], 0);
end;
```

This will create a simple pop-up dialog with the message **Hello World**, an **OK** button, and the icon that represents an informational message for the platform being used.

Compiling and running

As was done with the console application, compile the project by either using the main menu, that is, by going to **Run | Compile**, or use the keyboard shortcut *Ctrl + F9*. The following message appears in the the **Messages** window:

Project "project2" successfully built

Run the program by either using the main menu (**Run | Run**), or use the keyboard shortcut *F9*. You could also use the quick icon for **Run**, the green arrow. The application will start and the form will appear with `Button1`. Click on the button and the following dialog should appear:

Debugging

Bugs are part of the development process, and having successfully built a project with Lazarus, it is time to explore the debugger. With a program as simple as Hello World, there are very few places to make a mistake. Expanding on the Hello World application is necessary.

Expanding the Hello World application

Using **Form1**, from the **Standard** tab of the component palette, add three `TEdit` components, three `TLabel` components, and one `TButton`. From the **Additional** tab, add one **TSpeedButton**. From the **Dialogs** tab, add one **TCalendarDialog** to **Form1**.

Click on **Label1**. In the **Object Inspector** window, locate the the property **Caption**. Click on the current value of **Caption**, which is **Label1**, and change it to **First Name**. Follow the same procedure:

1. Change the caption **Label2** to **Last Name**.
2. Change caption **Label3** to **Date Of Birth**.
3. Change the caption **TSpeedButton** to "**...**" (without the quotes).
4. Change the caption **Button1** to **Execute**.
5. Change the caption **Button2 Caption** to **Exit**.

When completed, the form should look similar to the following screenshot:

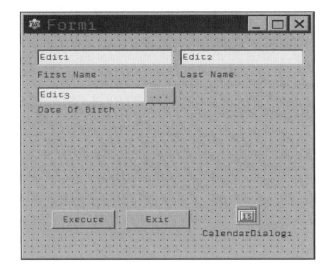

Double-click on **Button2**, and add the following code snippet to the **Button2Click** procedure:

```
Application.Terminate;
```

In the implementation section, add a new method called `GetUserName`:

```
function TForm1.GetUserName();
begin
  result Edit1.Text + ' ' + Edit2.Text;
end;
```

Modify the `Button1Click` method to read as follows:

```
procedure TForm1.Button1Click(Sender: TObject);
var
  UserName : String;
begin
  UserName := GetUserName();
  MessageDlg('Hello, ' + UserName, TMsgDlgType.mtInformation,
[TMsgDlgBtn.mbOK], 0);
end;
```

Save the changes and compile. Compilation should fail and an error similar to the following error should appear in the **Messages** window:

```
unit2.pas(42,23) Fatal: Syntax error, ":" expected but ";" found
```

Double-click on the error message, and the line in error will be highlighted in the **Source Editor** window. While examining the error, it can bee seen that the compiler was expecting to find a colon (:) next in the code, but instead a semicolon (;), which signals a line's end, was present. In the line of code, `GetUserName` is declared as a function, but no return type was given in the declaration. To correct that error, correct the line to read as follows:

```
function TForm1.GetUserName(): String;
```

Save and compile the code. The compilation should complete successfully this time. Run the program and fill in the **First Name** and **Last Name** textboxes, and click on the **Execute** button. The message in the pop-up dialog should now change to include the names entered.

Now add two more methods. First, double-click on the `TSpeedButton` on the form, and modify the procedure as follows:

```
procedure TForm1.SpeedButton1Click(Sender: TObject);
var
  DateString : String;
begin
  CalendarDialog1.Execute;
  DateTimeToString(DateString, 'mm/dd/yyyy', CalendarDialog1.Date);
  Edit3.Text := DateString;
end;
```

Next, declare a new private function called `CalculateAge` that returns a string value. Implement the function to read the date of birth from the `Edit3` textbox, and subtract today's date from that date:

```
function TForm1.CalculateAge(): String;
var
  DOB, Today, Age : TDateTime;
  AgeString : String;
begin
  dob := CalendarDialog1.Date;
  today := Now();
  Age := (today - dob);
  DateTimeToString(AgeString, 'mm/dd/yyyy', Age);

  result := AgeString;
end;
```

Before compiling the code, the unit `dateutils` must be added to the `uses` clause. Save and compile the changes. Run the program, fill in the name in the textboxes again, and click the **Speed** button, and the **Calendar** dialog will appear. Choose a date as the date of birth. Click on the **Execute** button, and a dialog box, similar to the following screenshot, will appear:

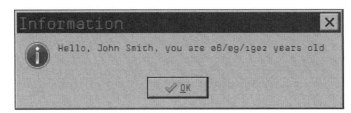

The age appears to be wrong, which means there is an error in the `CalculateAge` function. Running the code and placing a breakpoint in this method should be the next step. In the `CalculateAge` function, place a breakpoint in the first line of code:

```
dob := CalendarDialog1.Date;
```

Using the preceding code snippet, place the cursor on that line, right-click and highlight the **Debug** entry on the pop-up menu, and then select **Toggle Breakpoint**. Alternatively, the breakpoint can be set by pressing the *F5* key.

Run the program, and fill in the form as before. This time, when the **Execute** button is clicked, the program will stop running when it reaches the breakpoint.

Debugging commands

Examining some of the more commonly used debugging commands and shortcuts will make debugging the code much simpler:

- Step Over (*F8*): This command executes the code one statement at a time. If a method is encountered, do not enter into that code.

- Step Into (*F7*): This command executes the code one statement at a time. If a method is encountered, enter into the method's code, and execute the code one line at a time.

- Run To Cursor (*F4*): This command executes the code until the current position of the cursor is reached.

- Stop (*Ctrl* + *F4*): This command stops the execution of the code and exits the debugger.

- Evaluate/Modify (*Ctrl* + *F7*): This command shows the current result of an expression and modifies that expression, evaluates it, and shows the result.

- Inspect (*Alt* + *F5*): This command shows the type and value of a variable.

Since an age calculation is what this function is to perform, double-click on the Age variable to highlight it, and add it to the debug inspector by using the *Alt* + *F5* keyboard shortcut. The **Debug Inspector** window will appear as shown in the following screenshot:

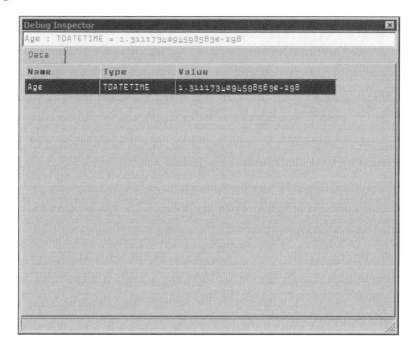

Since the Age variable line has not been reached by the debugger, the value seen in the preceding screenshot is from the initial creation of the Age variable. Press *F8* three times to reach the line after the assignment of a value to the Age variable. Notice that, in the **Debug Inspector** window, the value of **Age** has changed. The inspector shows us that age is TDateTime, which is how it was declared in the variable section of the function. Since Age only needs to be the number of years between two dates, the calculation of Age needs to be changed. Since this function does not actually calculate age, let's rename it GetAge. The easiest way to do this is to double-click on the function's name CalculateAge, and press *F2*. This will invoke the **Find** or **Rename Identifier** window. In the textbox, in the **Rename to** section, the current name will be present; change that to the new function name GetAge. Click on the **Rename all References** button. Using this method will rename the method everywhere it is found in the code, saving time and eliminating possible mistakes. Declare a new function, using the name CalculateAge, that takes two dates as its parameters and returns an integer representing the year. Use the following code as the implementation of the new function:

```
function TForm1.CalculateAge(DOB, Current: TDateTime): Integer;
var
  DobMonth, CurrentMonth, DobDay, CurrentDay, DobYear, CurrentYear :
word;
begin
    DecodeDate(DOB, DobYear, DobMonth, DobDay);
    DecodeDate(Current, CurrentYear, CurrentMonth, CurrentDay);

    if (DobYear = CurrentYear) and (DobMonth = CurrentMonth) and
(DobDay = CurrentDay) then
    begin
      Result := 0;
    end
    else
    begin
      Result := CurrentYear - DobYear;
      if (DobMonth > CurrentMonth) then
        Dec(Result)
      else
        begin
          if DobMonth = CurrentMonth then
            if (DobDay > CurrentDay) then
              Dec(Result);
        end;
    end;
end;
```

The line that assigns a value to the Age variable needs to be changed in the renamed GetAge function to:

```
Age := Calculate(dob, today);
```

Remove the line following this, as it is no longer needed. Change the last line of the function as follows:

```
result := IntToStr(Age);
```

Save the changes, compile, and run the application. This time, when stepping through the code using *F8*, the Age variable should be set to the age that is correct for the date of birth that was chosen. Press *F9*, and the application will continue, and dialog should appear with the correct message, as shown in the following screenshot:

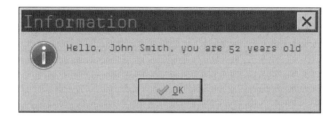

Other debugger features

There are a number of debugger features that were not used in the preceding example that can be useful. These can be accessed with keyboard shortcuts or by using the main menu (**View | Debug Windows**).

Press *Ctrl + Alt + W* to open the watches window. This window displays all variables and expressions that are on the current watch list. Items can be added to the watch list by clicking on a variable or highlighting an entire expression and using the keyboard shortcut *Ctrl + F5* or right-clicking and using the **Debug** entry of the pop-up menu.

Press *Ctrl + Alt + B* to open the breakpoints window. This window displays all the current breakpoints in the project, no matter if the unit is currently opened or not. The breakpoint can be enabled, disabled, or deleted by clicking on the breakpoint in the list, then selecting the appropriate icon from the toolbar or selecting it from the menu presented through right-clicking. Double-clicking on the breakpoint in the list will take you to the line of code in the **Source Editor** window. The unit containing the code will be automatically opened in the source-coded editor window if it is not currently opened, or it will be made the active window if it is not.

Press *Ctrl + Alt + R* to open the registers' window. If there is a need to see the content of a system register location, such as eax, ebx, or es, while debugging is in progress, then use this window to view them.

Press *Ctrl + Alt + L* to open the local variables window. This window shows all the variables and their values that are local to the method, which is currently used in the debugger when stepping through the code. The following screenshot shows the local variable window when stepping through the CalculateAge method that was created previously:

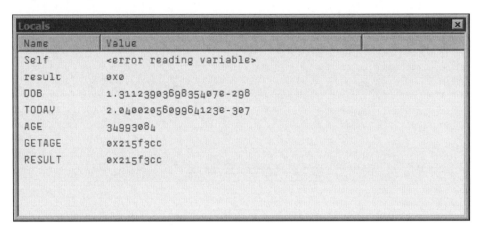

Deploying

The Lazarus integrated development environment does not provide a method to package and deploy applications it creates. There are various programs and methods to create distribution packages for the different platforms that Free Pascal and Lazarus support.

For Windows, there is Inno Setup (http://www.jrsoftware.org/isinfo.php), a free installer program that was written in Delphi, and its full source code is available as well. The Lazarus installer for Windows was created using this software.

Linux-based systems should use the package management system targeted for their distribution. For Debian-based systems, create .deb files. For systems that use the Red Hat package management system, create .rpm files.

For a more complete listing of programs and methods of creating installers and packages for different platforms, visit http://wiki.freepascal.org/Deploying_Your_Application.

Summary

In this chapter, we built a console version of the traditional Hello World application using the new application wizard of Lazarus. We examined the auto-generated source code that is created when using the wizard. We learned about the different sections of the source code, such as the uses clause, which listed the other units that are referenced. We also walked through the type section (where classes are declared) and the implementation section (where declared classes and methods are actually written). We, finally, learned how to compile and run the application by using the keyboard shortcut or using the main menu.

Also, we created a GUI version of the Hello World application and learned how to add components to a form. We learned that components added to a form are published properties of the form they are added to. We learned the keyword override and what that does to a method.

We expanded the GUI version of the application to learn about the debugging functions of Lazarus. We discovered how to place breakpoints in our source code and how to use the debugging keyboard shortcuts, such as Step Over, Step Into, and Run To.

Finally, we looked at the different third-party methods of deploying applications created with Lazarus, such as Inno Setup for Windows and the package managers for different distributions of Linux.

4
Converting Delphi

In this chapter, we will learn:

- The process of converting an existing Delphi project to a Lazarus project
- About using the Convert Delphi Project Wizard as well as the process of manually converting a Delphi project
- About the differences in Lazarus' LCL and the Delphi VCL, along with semantic and syntax differences between **Free Component Library** (**FPC**) and Delphi

Differences between Lazarus and Delphi components

As we have seen, Lazarus is very similar to Delphi, but it must be noted that Lazarus is not a clone of Delphi and that it is not 100 percent compatible with projects created using Delphi. One example of this is that Delphi component packages cannot be installed directly into the Lazarus IDE. Before converting a Delphi project to Lazarus, we need to be aware of some of the differences of the environments.

The Delphi VCL and the Lazarus LCL are both designed with component hierarchies for rapid application development, but they are not identical. The VCL provides non-visual components, such as `TDataSet` and `TQuery`, while the LCL provides only visual components. Classes such as those that provide access to databases are part of the FCL. The FCL is part of Free Pascal and contains only non-visual components and units, such as classes, which contain implementation of such Delphi classes as `TStream` and `TStringList`. Other units included in the FCL are:

- `base64`: This unit implements `base64` encoding/decoding streams
- `db`: This unit contains a `TDataset` implementation and `TDatabase` aware descendents

- `ddg_ds`: This unit contains a `TDataset` descendent for use with a flat file (file of record)
- `dom`: This unit contains a Free Pascal implementation of the W3 **Consortium Document Object Model (DOM)** specification
- `gettext`: This is a unit implementing the GNU gettext tools
- `htmldoc`: This unit includes DOM classes for HTML
- `inifiles`: This unit includes implementation of the `TInifile` class
- `iostream`: This unit includes implementation of a stream class used to access standard input, standard output, and standard error
- `mysqldb`: This unit includes the `TDataset` descendent class used to access a MySQL database
- `rtfpars`: This unit implements a **Rich Text Format (RTF)** parsing class
- `sh_pas`: This unit is a syntax-highlighting object for Pascal syntax
- `sh_xml`: This unit is a syntax-highlighting object for XML documents
- `xmlcfg`: This is a configuration unit that stores a configuration as an XML document
- `xmlread`: This is a unit to read an XML document and generate a DOM structure from it
- `xmlwrite`: This is a unit to take an XML document object and generate an XML file from it
- `zstream`: This is a unit that contains compression streams and streams to read `.gzipped` files

Not all controls that are found in the VCL are available in the LCL, and the same is true for some of the LCL controls. Although a control may be found in the LCL, that is, in the VCL, it is not a clone and changes will need to be made when porting Delphi code to Lazarus. Let's look at some of the major differences now.

Porting is the process of adapting software so an executable program can be created for a computing environment that is different from the one for which it was originally designed (for example, different CPU and operating systems). The term is also used when software or hardware is changed to make them usable in different environments.

Fonts

In the VCL, the use of specific fonts and font properties, such as bold or italics, is common and can be accessed through the Font or ParentFont property of a control. Setting these properties will not override the **Windows Appearance Theme** settings.

For the LCL, this cannot be true since the LCL is a cross-platform. The LCL will use the native Desktop or Toolkit appearance or theme on any control. For example, on a Mac, it will use the Cocoa setting natively; with the GTK toolkit, it will use the gtk theme; and with Windows, it will use the Windows native interface, unless another toolkit is specified. Only custom-drawn controls that are canvas-drawn can have the same level of customization as VCL controls. Custom-drawn controls, such as LCL-CustomDrawn-Anroid2, need backends that implement lower-level functions, such as the processing of messages and calling of events.

Lazarus Custom Drawn Controls are controls which draw themselves. Custom-drawn controls have the ability to fully customize the drawing, have exactly the same look in different platforms, and a higher consistency of behavior.

The custom-drawn controls, which are necessary for implementing Lazarus widget sets, are located in the unit lazarus/lcl/customdrawncontrols.pas.

All other custom-drawn controls are located in the package lazarus/components/customdrawn.

Dragging and docking

VCL controls allow for the dragging and docking of controls from one container control to another during runtime. Currently, the methods in the LCL TControl object that implement this functionality are available in the AnchorDocking package.

TEdit and TCustomEdit

The PasswordChar property does not work on all interfaces of the TEdit control. Alternatively, the EchoMode property of TCustomEdit should be set to emPassword when text should be hidden.

TCustomTreeView and TTreeView

The features of the LCL version of `TCustomView` and `TTreeView` are comparable to their VCL equivalent controls with their properties being compatible. Although the properties are compatible, the options for these properties may be named and act differently from their VCL counterparts. Some of the differences are:

- The LCL provides a `TCustomTreeView.Options` property that controls its behavior and appearance. These options are:

    - `tvoAllowMultiselect`: This option enables multi-node select mode, equivalent to enabling `TCustomTreeView.MultiSelect` in the VCL

    - `tvoAutoExpand`: These are auto-expand nodes, equivalent to enabling `TCustomTreeView.AutoExpand`

    - `tvoAutoInsertMark`: This option updates the drag preview on mouse move

    - `tvoAutoItemHeight`: This option adjusts the item heights automatically

    - `tvoHideSelection`: This option does not mark the selected item

    - `tvoHotTrack`: This option uses hot tracking, equivalent to enabling `TCustomTreeview.HotTrack`

    - `tvoKeepCollapsedNodes`: When shrinking/folding nodes, this option keeps the child nodes

    - `tvoReadOnly`: This option makes `Treeview` read-only, equivalent to enabling `TCustomTreeview.ReadOnly`

    - `tvoRightClickSelect`: This option allows using right-clicking on select nodes, equivalent to enabling `TCustomTreeView.RightClickSelect`

    - `tvoRowSelect`: This option allows selecting rows, equivalent to enabling `TCustomTreeView.RowSelect`

    - `tvoShowButtons`: This option shows buttons, equivalent to enabling `TCustomTreeView.ShowButtons`

    - `tvoShowLines`: This option shows node lines, equivalent to enabling `TCustomTreeView.ShowLines`

    - `tvoShowRoot`: This option shows root note, equivalent to enabling `TCustomTreeView.ShowRoot`

    - `tvoShowSeparators`: This option shows separators

    - `tvoToolTips`: This option shows tooltips for individual nodes

- The LCL provides the following additional properties:
  - ° `TCustomTreeView.OnSelectionChange` event
  - ° `TCustomTreeView.DefaultItems` for the default number of items
  - ° `TCustomTreeView.ExpandSignType` to determine the sign used on expandable/collapsible nodes

- While most `On Drag/Dock` events are available in the LCL, they do not work

Messages and events

The LCL implements messages and events, such as `OnShow`, `OnEnter`, and `OnActivate`, like the VCL counterparts, but they differ depending on the widget set. The LCL has a subset of Win API messages to ease the porting of Delphi components, but most work differently than the VCL counterparts. Delphi code that uses the Win API will most likely not work the same with the LCL and must be manually checked and converted. LCL messages start with the prefix LM instead of WM, for example, `LM_MOUSEENTER` instead of `WM_MOUSEENTER`.

Unit differences

Since the LCL is not specific to windows, the unit names in some cases are different from the VCL unit names. The following listing shows some of these differences:

- The VCL Windows unit corresponds to the `Interfaces`, `LCLIntf`, `LCLType`, and `LCLProc` units of the LCL. As Lazarus does not emulate the Win32 API, many of the functions differ. These functions exists so that Delphi code can be ported quickly. The `Interfaces` unit needs to be included in the `.lpr` file to initialize the appropriate widgetset.

- The `LMessages` unit of the LCL implements the Win32 event callbacks of the `TControl` messages found in the `Messages` unit of the VCL.

- Some types found in the `Graphics` and `Controls` units of Delphi are included in the LCL unit named `GraphType`.

- The `MaskEdit` unit of the LCL corresponds to the `Mask` unit of Delphi and contains the `TMaskEdit` class.

Conversion methods

Delphi projects can be converted either manually or using the Delphi Converter wizard in Lazarus. Before beginning the conversion process, we need to note some considerations and information.

Filenames and extension

Filenames are case-sensitive on some file systems. When converting Delphi filenames, you should make your filename lowercase to avoid **File Not Found** error messages.

Lazarus and Delphi use different file extensions for corresponding units. The following table shows the correlation between the different file extension types:

Delphi	Description	Lazarus	Description
.pas	Delphi source file	.pas, .pp	Pascal unit file
.dfm	Delphi form	.lfm	Form data file
.dcu	Delphi compiled unit	.o, .ppu	Compiled unit
.dpr	Delphi project	.lpr	Project file
.res	Windows resource file	N/A	
.dof	Delphi option file	N/A	
		.lrs	Lazarus resource file
		.lpi	Lazarus project information
		.ppu	FPC unit description file

Semantic and syntax differences

Parameter evaluation in Delphi is guaranteed to be from left-hand side to right-hand side. Free Pascal can evaluate parameters in any order so that the code generated is optimized.

The Free Pascal compiler supports different compiler modes that are set using compiler directives. Among them, there is Delphi compatibility mode, which is set by using the {$Mode DELPHI} directive and OBJFPC mode. The use of {$Mode OBJFPC} is the recommended mode to use, as it has a more strict syntax checking.

The following syntax changes should always be followed when converting Delphi code when using the {$Mode ObjFPC} directive:

```
Prefix event handler methods with an "@"
```

For example, a button callback in Delphi has the following code:

```
begin
  if not Assigned(ThisButton.OnClick) then
    ThisButton.OnClick := CallThisFunction;
end;
```

The Free Pascal conversion should be as follows:

```
begin
  if not Assigned(ThisButton.OnClick) then
    ThisButton.OnClick := @CallThisFunction;
end;
```

When calling a function, you must append the parenthesis to the function name.

In Delphi, there is no difference between a function result and a variable, but there is this distinction in Free Pascal. For example, in Delphi:

```
With (ThisObject) do
begin
  If Assigned(OnCallBack) then
    OnCallBack;
  end;
The Free Pascal equivalent is as follows:
With (ThisObject) do
begin
  If Assigned(OnCallBack) then
    OnCallBack();
  end;
```

The pointer to record values must be de-referenced.

Delphi does not require the de-referencing of a point to a value in a record. Delphi treats the point as if it were the record. This is not true for Free Pascal, and the pointer must be de-referenced.

The Delphi code is as follows:

```
Function GetRecordValue(ARecord: PMyRecord):Integer;
begin
  If Assigned(ARecord) then
    Result:=ARecord.AValue
  else
    Result:=0;
end;
```

The Free Pascal Conversion is as follows:

```
Function GetRecordValue(ARecord: PMyRecord):Integer;
begin
  If Assigned(ARecord) then
    Result:=ARecord^.AValue
  else
    Result:=0;
end;
```

When indexing a string property of an object, it must be enclosed in parentheses.

In Delphi, it is possible to treat an object property as if it were a constant or variable. Doing so allows individual characters (chars) to be accessed by indexing a property of the type string. In Free Pascal code, the string property should be enclosed in parentheses.

The Delphi code is as follows:

```
Type TMyComponent=class(TComponent).
  .
  .
Published
  Property StringProperty:String index 3 read GetStringProperty;
End;

var
  CharVariable :char;
begin
  If Length(StringProperty)>2 then
    CharVariable := StringProperty[3];
end;
```

The Free Pascal Conversion is as follows:

```
Type TMyComponent=class(TComponent)   .
  .
  .
Published
  Property StringProperty:String index 3 read GetStringProperty;
End;

var
  CharVariable :char;
begin
  If Length(StringProperty)>2 then
    CharVariable := (StringProperty)[3];
end;
```

Pointers must be typecast when used with `function` or `var`.

Delphi allows for null pointer variable to represent an object; this is done as a method to prevent circular referencing of units. Because of this, it is possible to send a null pointer to a function that expects an `object` type as a parameter without typecasting.

The Delphi code is as follows:

```
Unit 1
  Type
    TObjectOne = class(TComponent)
    End;

  Procedure DoSomething(Value: TObjectOne);
  Function GetObjectOne: TObjectOne;

Unit 2
  Type
    TMyComponent=class(TComponent)
    Published ObjectPointer: Pointer;
  End;

Application
var
  MyComponent: TMyComponent;
begin
  MyComponent.ObjectPointer := GetObjectOne;
  DoSomething(MyComponent.ObjectPointer);
end;
```

The Free Pascal Conversion is as follows:

```
Unit 1
  Type
    TObjectOne = class(TComponent)
    End;

  Procedure DoSomething(Value: TObjectOne);
  Function GetObjectOne: TObjectOne;

Unit 2
  Type
    TMyComponent=class(TComponent)
    Published ObjectPointer: Pointer;
  End;
```

```
Application
var
  MyComponent: TMyComponent;
begin
  MyComponent.ObjectPointer := Pointer(GetObjectOne);
  DoSomething(TObjectOne(MyComponent.ObjectPointer));
end;
```

32-bit and 64-bit considerations

A 64-bit pointer requires 8 bytes, whereas a 32-bit pointer requires only 4 bytes. Since the `integer` type is 32 bit, you cannot typecast pointers to integers or integers to pointers. Free Pascal defines two types to solve this problem:

- `PtrInt` a 32-bit signed integer on 32-bit platforms and a 64-bit signed integer on 64-bit platforms
- `PtrUInt` unsigned integer on both 64-bit and 32-bit platforms

If your code needs to be Delphi compatible, add the following compiler directive to handle this:

```
{$IFNDEF FPC}
type
  PtrInt = integer;
  PtrUInt = cardinal;
{$ENDIF}
```

Resource files

Since resource files (`.res`) are specific to the Win32 platform, they are not compatible with Lazarus and will need to be recreated and compiled using Lazres. Lazres is located in the Lazarus tools subdirectory. The command line for using Lazres is as follows:

```
lazres resource_file_name  [resources...]
```

For example, if you wanted to add two PNG files to a resource file named `images`, use the command line as follows:

```
lazres  images.lrs one.png two.png
```

To use a resource file in a unit, you must:

- Add the `LResources` unit to the `uses` clause
- Add a resource file to the initialization block of the unit using the `{$I}` compiler directive, such as `{$I images.lrs}`

Using the Convert Delphi Project Wizard

Let's now look at converting an existing Delphi application by using the Convert Delphi Project Wizard. We are going to use a simple program called DRU, the Delimiter Replacement Utility, which you can download from `http://www.rodperson.com/DL/lazarus/dru.zip`. As implied by the name, the application looks for a character in a text file that is used as a delimiter for that file; the user chooses another character to replace that delimiter and saves the file to another text file. This program was originally created because of a business need that required flat text files to use the pipe character (|), but some of the clients that submitted files were unable to generate such a file and could only supply files that used commas (,) as the delimiter. Although it would seem an easy change of a program on the client's end, the DRU program has actually come in many times over the years. Once the package is downloaded, unzip the file in a directory of your choice. In that directory, create another directory called `Convert`. To this directory copy, the following files:

- `DRU.dcu`
- `DRU.ddp`
- `DRU.dfm`
- `DRU_2007.pas`
- `DRU_2007.dpr`
- `DRU.res`
- `test-in.csv`

The file `test-in.csv` is a test file that we will open to convert. In the directory, you unzipped the package to a file called `out.csv`, which is the correct output of the Delphi version of the program. We will use that for comparison; after running the version, we will create it with Lazarus.

Now that we have the project ready for conversion, bring up the project wizard by closing the current project:

1. Select **Convert Delphi Project** from the **Tools** menu.

2. Browse to the `convert` subdirectory we created and select the file `DRU.dpr`.

3. The **Project Conversion Wizard Option** dialog will appear. Set the following options:
    - **Unit Replacement: Interactive**
    - **Unknown properties: Interactive**
    - **Type Replacements: Interactive**
    - **Function Replacements: Enabled**
    - **Coordinate offsets: Enabled**
    - **Target**: Check the **Multi-Platform** checkbox
    - Check the **Make backup of changed files** checkbox

4. The option dialog should look like a 32-bit signed interger on 32-bit platforms. Click on the **Start Conversion** button.

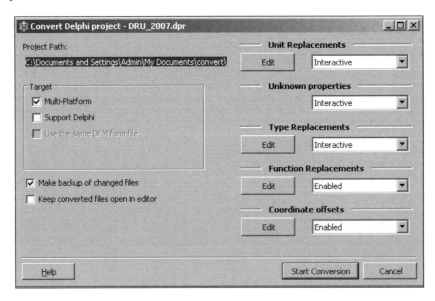

Because we have chosen interactive conversion, the process will begin first with the **Units to replace** dialog window appearing. This dialog will show the name of the Delphi VCL unit on the left-hand side. On the right-side, Lazarus LCL unit(s) that will replace each VCL unit will be listed. In the case of this application, only the Windows unit of the VCL will be replaced. As mentioned earlier, it will be replaced by the LCL units, such as LCLIntf, LCLType, and LMessages. Click on the **OK** button to continue.

Next, the **Fix LFM File** dialog window will appear. This dialog will show us the properties of the Delphi form that are not supported in Lazarus and will give us the option to either replace or remove them. In this case, two properties will be highlighted in the **OldCreateOrder** and **TextHeight** (next screenshot) dialog. We will just remove these two properties from the form since there is no equivalent property for a Lazarus form. Click on the button labeled **Fix unknown properties and types**.

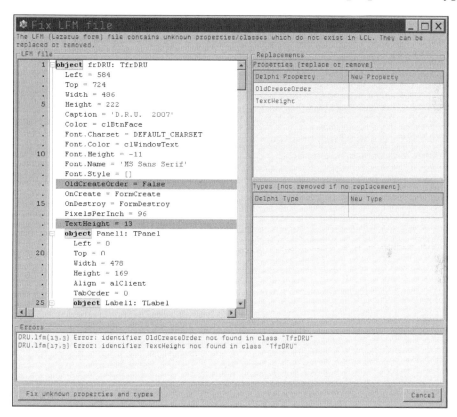

When the conversion process has completed, the **Source File Editor** window will appear with DRU_2007.lpr opened, and the **Messages** window will display information about the conversion process and that the converted project is ready for use. Since the conversion process completed successfully and all seems to be in order, save the project by clicking on the **Save All** quick icon. Now compile the project by either using the keyboard shortcut *Ctrl + F9* or selecting **Compile** from the **Run** menu.

Before we run the Lazarus-created version of the application, let's look at the correct version created by Delphi. Browse to the directory that you unzipped the downloaded package to and run DRU_2007.exe. The screenshot that follows is what the correct Delphi version of the application should look like. Take a minute to hover over the buttons on the bottom of the application and notice the hints that appear.

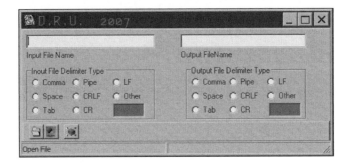

We can now run the program and see what it does by doing the following:

1. Click on the **Open File** button, and choose the test-in.csv file.
2. Click on the **Save File** button, choose a destination directory, and name the file out-delphi.csv.
3. Click on the **Replace Delimiter** button.

The application should not take long to transform the delimiters and create the new file. When execution is complete, the status bar will show the message "**Done Processing File. Awaiting Command**" in the first pane and the total processing time in the second pane, as shown in the following screenshot:

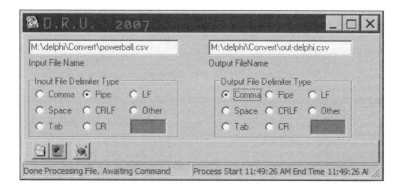

Now that we have seen how the Delphi version looks and performs, we can now return to Lazarus and run the version compile with it. Run the program by pressing *F9* or using the **Run** menu. The first thing you will notice is that the application looks a little different from the Delphi version. The status bar does not contain separate panes. The form is longer and contains a gap above the buttons and the delimiter radio button groups. And finally, if you hover over the buttons, there are no hints that appear.

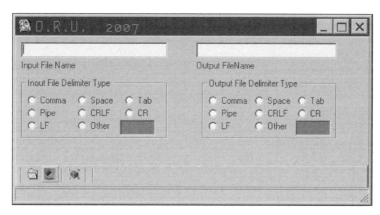

Before we make any changes to the application's appearance, let's run the program and see how it compares to the Delphi compiled version. Again, open the file `test-in.csv`. This time, save the file as `out-laz.csv`, and click on the **Replace Delimiters** button. Did you notice anything different? When you ran the Lazarus compiled version, there were no messages whatsoever on the signal that the application has completed its operations on the file. The only way to tell is to look in the directory chosen for output and see if the file is present.

Essentially, the application conversion did complete successfully and is fully functional, we just need to make the application as user-friendly as the Delphi version. To do this, we need to add the hints for the buttons and the messages on the status bar, using the following procedure:

1. Open the **View Project Forms** dialog by using *Ctrl + F2* or through the **Project** menu.

2. Select **frDRU** in the dialog, as it should be the only form available, and click on **OK**. The source code for the DRU.pas will appear in the **Source Editor** window.

3. In the **Object Inspector Component Tree** window, click on the **tbtbnOpenFile** node. The **Open File** button will now be highlighted on the form.

4. On the **Properties** tab, find the Hint property. Notice that the Hint property does contain the value Open File, which means another property is keeping the hint from being shown when the button is hovered over.

5. There are two other properties that relate to showing hints, ParentShowHint, which will use the ShowHint property of the parent container, and ShowcHint, which can be set to explicitly show or not show the hint of the component despite the parent property setting.

6. Let's set the ShowHint property to True.

Repeat this procedure for the tbtnSaveFile and tbtnRun buttons.

 If the form does not appear, press the *F12* key.

Next, we need to determine why the messages on the status bar that appear in the Delphi version of the application do not appear in the Lazarus version. The messages are written to the status bar before and after the delimiters have all been replaced, and the new file is saved. This occurs in the procedure tBtnRunClick. In the DRU. pas unit, find this procedure. The procedure should look like the following code:

```
procedure TfrDRU.tBtnRunClick(Sender: TObject);
var
   starttime,endtime : TDateTime;
begin
```

```
    Statusbar1.Panels[0].Text := 'Replace all ' + Delimiter + 's with '
+ ReplaceWith;
    Refresh;
    Starttime := NOW;
    ReplaceDelimiters(edtInputFile.FileName, FALSE, Delimiter,
ReplaceWith);
    EndTime := NOW;
    StatusBar1.Panels[0].Text := 'Done Processing File. Awaiting
Command';
    Statusbar1.Panels[1].Text := 'Process Start ' + TimeToStr(StartTime)
+ ' End Time ' + TimeToStr(EndTime);
    end;
```

You can see the code lines for writing messages to the status bar are present. Since the program compiles, this means that there must be a property of the TStatusBar set, which either has a different default setting in Delphi or does not exist. If you recall the messages that were shown during the conversion, you may have noticed a message that the property SimplePanel was added to Statusbar1. Select the status bar on the form and locate the SimplePanel property in the **Object Inspector** window, and set it to False. Run the application. The hints should appear when hovering over the buttons, and the status bar will display the messages sent to it.

You may have also noticed that the separator buttons are visible on the toolbar. This can be changed by setting the **Visible** property to **False** on the button with the **Style** property set to tbsSeparator. Finally, you can resize the form by hovering over the lower-right corner until the double-headed diagonal arrow cursor appears. Hold the left mouse button down and drag the form to the new desired size.

The conversion process is the same regardless of which platform you are using Lazarus on. The code for the DRU application can be converted on a non-Windows platform, as there is nothing specific to Windows or the Win32 API contained in the code. If you were to convert a Windows project with units that could not be converted to an equivalent unit in the LCL, you would be presented with the **Unit not found** dialog windows—an example of which can be seen in the screenshot that follows. This example shows four different units that cannot be converted automatically. The first unit is a custom component called CCBHLogin that is used to validate user credentials against a database.

Next is ADODB. This is the unit to access the ActiveX data objects for database, and since ActiveX is Windows-only, there is no direct converts in the LCL.

The last two units are part of the Project JEDI's JVCL3. Project JEDI is an open source library and set of components for Delphi, but, due to the reliance on Win32 and some internals of Delphi, many of the components will not work with Lazarus directly and are in need of converting themselves.

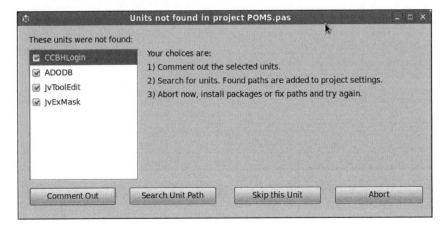

When a unit cannot be converted automatically, you have the option to comment out that unit, search for the unit, skip the unit, or abort the conversion process. Comment out the unit only comments out the unit in the uses clause. Any code that uses a class or method defined in that unit will need to be commented out or converted manually. If you choose to skip the unit, then nothing will be done at all to the unit and all conversion must be done manually, as this will involve the porting of the source code.

The process porting can be complex. Porting can involve as little as changing the name of a type to totally rewriting a unit's code. The porting of code is a process that takes time and practice and is beyond the scope of this book.

Converting a Delphi project manually

If you have a simple Delphi project that you know will not involve porting of the code, you may wish to manually convert it to a Lazarus project by following these steps:

1. Make a copy of the Delphi project in a new directory.

2. Rename all .dfm files to .lfm.

3. Rename the .dpr file to .lpr.

4. Make these changes to the `.lpr` file as needed:

    i.   Add `{$mode delphi}{$H+}` or `{$mode objfpc}{H+}` directives.

    ii. Add `Interfaces` to the `uses` clause.

    iii. Remove `{$R *.res}` directive by commenting or deleting.

5. Make needed changes to all `.pas` unit files:

    i.   Add `{$mode delphi}{$H+}` or `{$mode objfpc}{H+}` directives.

    ii. Add `LResources` to the `uses` clause.

    iii. Add `buttons` to the `uses` clause if the form has buttons.

    iv. Remove the `{$R *.dfm}` directive.

    v.   Add an initialization section at the end of each unit file.

    vi. Add `{$I unitname.lrs}` directive to each initialization section.

6. Select **New Project** from the **Project** menu.

7. Select the `.lpr` file.

8. In the **Create a new project** dialog, choose **Application**.

9. Build the project.

10. Correct any errors that are shown during the build process:

    ○   The `.lpi` file is generated automatically

    ○   If **Error reading Form** messages appear, click on **Continue Loading**

11. Save all.

Now, you have a Lazarus project.

Summary

In this chapter, we learned how to convert a Delphi project using the Convert Delphi Project Wizard, as well as a brief overview of the manual process of converting. We saw that, when converting, we need to be aware of the differences between Delphi's VCL and the Lazarus LCL. We also need to take into consideration whether the converted project will be cross-compiled for different platforms. We learned that there are some differences between 32-bit and 64-bit types.

In the next chapter, we will learn how to create a component for Lazarus.

5
Creating a Lazarus Component

In this chapter, we are going to look at creating new components for Lazarus. We will do this by:

- Creating a message-logging component
- Adding properties to the components that appear in the **Object Inspector** window when a component is used in design time
- Adding events of the components that appear in the **Object Inspector** window when a component is used in design time
- Learning the basics of creating a **Property Editor** window
- Learning the basics of creating a **Component Editor** window and looking at the TCheckListBoxComponentEditor component are some examples

So let's begin.

Creating a new component package

We are going to create a custom-logging component, and add it to the **Misc** tab of the component palette. To do this, we first need to create a new package and add out component to that package along with any other required resources, such as an icon for the component. To create a new package, do the following:

1. Select **package** from the main menu.
2. Select **New Package....** from the submenu.
3. Select a directory that appears in the **Save** dialog and create a new directory called MyComponents. Select the MyComponents directory.
4. Enter MyComponents as the filename and press the **Save** button.

Now, you have a new package that is ready to have components added to it. Follow these steps:

1. On the **Package** dialog window, click on the add (+) button.

2. Select the **New Component** tab.

3. Select **TComponent** as **Ancestor Type**.

4. Set **New class name** to **TMessageLog**.

5. Set **Palette Page** to **Misc**.

6. Leave all the other settings as they are.

You should now have something similar to the following screenshot. If so, click on the **Create New Component** button:

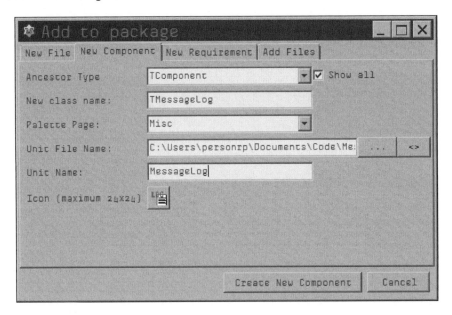

You should see **messagelog.pas** listed under the **Files** node in the **Package** dialog window. Let's open this file and see what the auto-generated code contains. Double-click on the file or choose **Open file** from **More menu** in the **Package** dialog.

 Do not name your component the same as the package. This will cause you problems when you compile the package later. If you were to do this, the .pas file would be over written, because the compile procedure creates a .pas file for the package automatically.

The code in the **Source Editor** window is given as follows:

```
unit TMessageLog;
{$mode objfpc}{$H+}
interface
uses
  Classes, SysUtils, LResources, Forms, Controls, Graphics, Dialogs,
StdCtrls;
type
  TMessageLog = class(TComponent)
  private
    { Private declarations }
  protected
    { Protected declarations }
  public
    { Public declarations }
  published
    { Published declarations }
  end;
procedure Register;
implementation
procedure Register;
begin
  RegisterComponents('Misc',[TMessageLog]);
end;
end.
```

What should stand out in the auto-generated code is the global procedure
`RegisterComponents`. `RegisterComponents` is contained in the `Classes` unit.
The procedure registers the component (or components if you create more than
one in the unit) to the component page that is passed to it as the first parameter of
the procedure.

Since everything is in order, we can now compile the package and install the
component.

Click the **Compile** button on the toolbar.

Once the compile procedure has been completed, select **Install**, which is located in the menu under the **Use** button. You will be presented with a dialog telling you that Lazarus needs to be rebuilt. Click on the **Yes** button, as shown in the following screenshot:

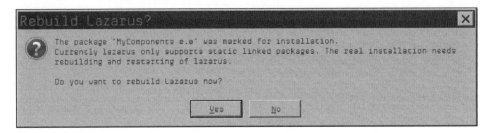

The Lazarus rebuilding process will take some time. When it is complete, it will need to be restarted. If this does not happen automatically, then restart Lazarus yourself.

On restarting Lazarus, select the **Misc** tab on the component palette. You should see the new component as the last component on the tab, as shown in the following screenshot:

You have now successfully created and installed a new component. You can now create a new application and add this component to a Lazarus form. The component in its current state does not perform any action. Let us now look at adding properties and events to the component that will be accessible in the **Object Inspector** window at design time.

Adding properties

Properties of a component that you would like to have visible in the **Object Inspector** window must be declared as published. Properties are attributes that determine an object's status and behavior. A property is a name that is mapped to read and write methods or access data directly. This means, when you read or write a property, you are accessing a field or calling a method of the object. For example, let us add a `FileName` property to `TMessageLog`, which is the name of the file that messages will be written to. The actual field of the object that will store this data will be named `fFileName`.

To the `TMessageLog` private declaration section, add:

```
fFileName: String;
```

To the `TMessagLog` published declaration section, add:

```
property FileName: String read fFileName write fFileName;
```

With these changes, when the packages are compiled and installed, the property `FileName` will be visible in the **Object Inspector** window when the `TMessageLog` declaration is added to a form in a project. You can do this now if you would like to verify this.

Adding events

Any interaction that a user has with a component, such as clicking it, generates an event. Events are also generated by the system in response to a method call or a change in a component's property, or if different component's property changes, such as the focus being set on one component causes the current component in focus to lose it, which triggers an event call. Event handlers are methods of the form containing the component; this technique is referred to as delegation. You will notice that when you double-click on a component's event in the object inspector it creates a new procedure of the form.

Events are properties, and such methods are assigned to event properties, as we just saw with normal properties. Because events are the properties and use of delegation, multiple events can share the same event handler.

The simplest way to create an event is to define a method of the type TNotifyEvent. For example, if we want to add an OnChange event to TMessageLog, we could add the following code:

```
...
private
  FonChange : TNotifyEvent;
  ...
public
  property OnChange: TNotifyEvent read FOnChange write FOnChange;
  ...
end;
```

When you double-click on the OnChange event in **Object Inspector**, the following method stub would be created in the form containing the TMessageLog component:

```
procedure TForm.MessageLogChange(Sender: TObject);
begin

end;
```

Some properties, such as OnChange or OnFocus, are sometimes called on the change of value of a component's property or the firing of another event. Traditionally, in this case, a method with the prefix of Do and with the suffix of the On event are called. So, in the case of our OnChange event, it would be called from the DoChange method (as called by some other method). Let us assume that, when a filename is set for the TMessageLog component, the procedure SetFileName is called, and that calls DoChange. The code would look as follows:

```
procedure SetFileName(name : string);
begin
  FFileName = name;
  //fire the event
  DoChange;
end;

procedure DoChange;
begin
  if Assigned(FOnChange) then
      FOnChange(Self);
end;
```

The `DoChange` procedure checks to see if anything has been assigned to the `FOnChange` field. If it is assigned, then it executes what is assigned to it. What this means is that if you double-click on the `OnChange` event in **Object Inspector**, it assigns the method name you enter to `FOnChange`, and this is the method that is called by `DoChange`.

Events with more parameters

You probably noticed that the `OnChange` event only had one parameter, which was `Sender` and is of the type `Object`. Most of the time, this is adequate, but there may be times when we want to send other parameters into an event. In those cases, `TNotifyEvent` is not an adequate type, and we will need to define a new type. The new type will need to be a method pointer type, which is similar to a procedural type but has the keyword of `object` at the end of the declaration. In the case of `TMessageLog`, we may need to perform some action before or after a message is written to the file. To do this, we will need to declare two method pointers, `TBeforeWriteMsgEvent` and `TAfterWriteMsgEvent`, both of which will be triggered in another method named `WriteMessage`. The modification of our code will look as follows:

```
type
  TBeforeWriteMsgEvent = procedure(var Msg: String; var OKToWrite:
Boolean) of Object;
  TAfterWriteMsgEvent = procedure(Msg: String) of Object;
TmessageLog = class(TComponent)
...
public
function WriteMessage(Msg: String): Boolean;
...
published
 property OnBeforeWriteMsg: TBeforeWriteMsgEvent read fBeforeWriteMsg
write fBeforeWriteMsg;
    property OnAfterWriteMsg: TAfterWriteMsgEvent read fAfterWriteMsg
write fAfterWriteMsg;
end;
implementation
function TMessageLog.WriteMessage(Msg: String): Boolean;
var
  OKToWrite: Boolean;
begin
  Result := FALSE;
  OKToWrite := TRUE;
```

```
    if Assigned(fBeforeWriteMsg) then
      fBeforeWriteMsg(Msg, OKToWrite);
    if OKToWrite then
    begin
      try
        AssignFile(fLogFile, fFileName);
        if FileExists(fFileName) then
          Append(fLogFile)
        else
          ReWrite(fLogFile);
        WriteLn(fLogFile, DateTimeToStr(Now()) + ' - ' + Msg);
        if Assigned(fAfterWriteMsg) then
          fAfterWriteMsg(Msg);
        Result := TRUE;
        CloseFile(fLogFile);
      except
        MessageDlg('Cannot write to log file, ' + fFileName + '!',
  mtError, [mbOK], 0);
        CloseFile(fLogFile);
      end; // try...except
    end; // if
end; // WriteMessage
```

While examining the function `WriteMessage`, we see that, before the `Msg` parameter is written to the file, the `FBeforeWriteMsg` field is checked to see if anything is assigned to it, and, if so, the `write` method of that field is called with the parameters `Msg` and `OKToWrite`. The method pointer `TBeforeWriteMsgEvent` declares both of these parameters as `var` types. So if any changes are made to the method, the changes will be returned to `WriteMessage` function. If the `Msg` parameter is successfully written to the file, the `FAfterWriteMsg` parameter is checked for assigned and executed parameter (if it is). The file is then closed and the function's result is set to `True`. If the `Msg` parameter value is not able to be written to the file, then an error dialog is shown, the file is closed, and the function's result is set to `False`.

With the changes that we have made to the `TMessageLog` unit, we now have a functional component. You can now save the changes, recompile, reinstall the package, and try out the new component by creating a small application using the `TMessageLog` component.

Property editors

Property editors are custom dialogs for editing special properties of a component. The standard property types, such as strings, images, or enumerated types, have default property editors, but special property types may require you to write custom property editors.

Custom property editors must extend from the class TPropertyEditor or one of its descendant classes. Property editors must be registered in the Register procedure using the function RegisterPropertyEditor from the unit PropEdits. An example of property editor class declaration is given as follows:

```
TPropertyEditor = class
  public
    function   AutoFill: Boolean; Virtual;
    procedure Edit; Virtual; // double-clicking the property value to
activate
    procedure ShowValue; Virtual; //control-clicking the property
value to activate
    function   GetAttributes: TPropertyAttributes; Virtual;
    function   GetEditLimit: Integer; Virtual;
    function   GetName: ShortString; Virtual;
    function   GetHint(HintType: TPropEditHint; x, y: integer): String;
Virtual;
    function   GetDefaultValue: AnsiString; Virtual;
    function   SubPropertiesNeedsUpdate: Boolean; Virtual;
    function   IsDefaultValue: Boolean; Virtual;
    function   IsNotDefaultValue: Boolean; Virtual;
    procedure GetProperties(Proc: TGetPropEditProc); Virtual;
    procedure GetValues(Proc: TGetStrProc); Virtual;
    procedure SetValue(const NewValue: AnsiString); Virtual;
    procedure UpdateSubProperties; Virtual;
  end;
```

Having a class as a property of a component is a good example of a property that would need a custom property editor. Because a class has many fields with different formats, it is not possible for Lazarus to have the object inspector make these fields available for editing without a property editor created for a class property, as with standard type properties. For such properties, Lazarus shows the property name in parentheses followed by a button with an ellipsis (…) that activates the property editor. This functionality is handled by the standard property editor called TClassPropertyEditor, which can then be inherited to create a custom property editor, as given in the following code:

```
TClassPropertyEditor = class(TPropertyEditor)
public
  constructor Create(Hook: TPropertyEditorHook; APropCount: Integer);
Override;
  function GetAttributes: TPropertyAttributes; Override;
  procedure GetProperties(Proc: TGetPropEditProc); Override;
  function GetValue: AnsiString; Override;
  property SubPropsTypeFilter: TTypeKinds Read FSubPropsTypeFilter
                                          Write SetSubPropsTypeFilter
                                          Default tkAny;
end;
```

Using the preceding class as a base class, all you need to do to complete a property editor is add a dialog in the Edit method as follows:

```
TMyPropertyEditor = class(TClassPropertyEditor)
  public
    procedure Edit; Override;
    function  GetAttributes: TPropertyAttributes; Override;
  end;

procedure TMyPropertyEditor.Edit;
var
  MyDialog: TCommonDialog;
begin
  MyDialog := TCommonDialog.Create(NIL);
  try
    ...
    //Here you can set attributes of the dialog
    MyDialog.Options := MyDialog.Options + [fdShowHelp];
    . . .
  finally
    MyDialog.Free;
  end;
end;
```

Component editors

Component editors control the behavior of a component when double-clicked or right-clicked in the form designer. Classes that define a component editor must descend from TComponentEditor or one of its descendent classes. The class should be registered in the Register procedure using the function RegisterComponentEditor. Most of the methods of TComponentEditor are inherited from it's ancestor TBaseComponentEditor, and, if you are going to write a component editor, you need to be aware of this class and its methods. Declaration of TBaseComponentEditor is as follows:

```
TBaseComponentEditor = class
  protected
  public
    constructor Create(AComponent: TComponent;
                       ADesigner: TComponentEditorDesigner); Virtual;
    procedure Edit; Virtual; Abstract;
    procedure ExecuteVerb(Index: Integer); Virtual; Abstract;
    function  GetVerb(Index: Integer): String; Virtual; Abstract;
    function  GetVerbCount: Integer; Virtual; Abstract;
```

```
    procedure PrepareItem(Index: Integer; const AnItem: TMenuItem);
Virtual; Abstract;
    procedure Copy; Virtual; Abstract;
    function  IsInInlined: Boolean; Virtual; Abstract;
    function  GetComponent: TComponent; Virtual; Abstract;
    function  GetDesigner: TComponentEditorDesigner; Virtual;
Abstract;
    function  GetHook(out Hook: TPropertyEditorHook): Boolean;
Virtual; Abstract;
    procedure Modified; Virtual; Abstract;
  end;
```

Let us look at some of the more important methods of the class.

The Edit method is called on the double-clicking of a component in the form designer.

GetVerbCount and GetVerb are called to build the context menu that is invoked by right-clicking on the component. A verb is a menu item. GetVerb returns the name of the menu item. GetVerbCount gets the total number of items on the context menu. The PrepareItem method is called for each menu item after the menu is created, and it allows the menu item to be customized, such as adding a submenu or hiding the item by setting its visibility to False. ExecuteVerb executes the menu item.

The Copy method is called when the component is copied to the clipboard.

A good example of a component editor is the TCheckListBox component editor. It is a descendant from TComponentEditor so all the methods of the TBaseComponentEditor do not need to be implemented. TComponentEditor provides empty implementation for most methods and sets defaults for others. Using this, methods that are needed for the TCheckListBoxComponentEditor component are overwritten. An example of the TCheckListBoxComponentEditor code is given as follows:

```
TCheckListBoxComponentEditor = class(TComponentEditor)
  protected
    procedure DoShowEditor;
  public
    procedure ExecuteVerb(Index: Integer); override;
    function GetVerb(Index: Integer): String; override;
    function GetVerbCount: Integer; override;
  end;
procedure TCheckGroupComponentEditor.DoShowEditor;
var
  Dlg: TCheckGroupEditorDlg;
begin
```

```
    Dlg := TCheckGroupEditorDlg.Create(NIL);
    try
      // .. shortened
      Dlg.ShowModal;
      // .. shortened
    finally
      Dlg.Free;
    end;
end;

procedure TCheckGroupComponentEditor.ExecuteVerb(Index: Integer);
begin
  case Index of
    0: DoShowEditor;
  end;
end;

function TCheckGroupComponentEditor.GetVerb(Index: Integer): String;
begin
  Result := 'CheckBox Editor...';
end;

function TCheckGroupComponentEditor.GetVerbCount: Integer;
begin
  Result := 1;
end;
```

Summary

In this chapter, we learned how to create a new Lazarus package and add a new component to that using the **New Package** dialog window to create our own custom component, TMessageLog. We also learned about compiling and installing a new component into the IDE, which requires Lazarus to rebuild itself in order to do so. Moreover, we discussed component properties. Then, we became acquainted with the events, which are triggered by any interaction that a user has with a component, such as clicking it, or by a system response, which could be caused by the change in any component of a form that affects another component. We studied that Events are properties, and they are handled through a technique called delegation. We discovered the simplest way to create an event is to create a descendant of TNotifyEvent — if you needed to send more parameters to an event and a single parameter provided by TNotifyEvent, then you need to declare a method pointer.

We learned that property editors are custom dialogs for editing special properties of a component that aren't of a standard type, such as string or integer, and that they must extend from TPropertyEditor. Then, we discussed the component editors, which control the behavior of a component when it is right-clicked or double-clicked in the form designer, and that a component editor must descend from TComponentEditor or a descendant class of it. Finally, we looked at an example of a component editor for the TCheckListBox.

Next, we will learn how to create documentation for our Lazarus projects.

6
The Lazarus
Documentation Editor

In this chapter we are going to learn about documenting our source code. We will do this by:

- Building the LazDE tool
- Opening the existing Lazarus documentation
- Creating documentation for our source code
- Using FPDoc to create documentation

Building the LazDE tool

The **Lazarus Documentation Editor (LazDE)** tool is developed to create platform-independent documentation of Lazarus source code units. XML files are used to record and store documentation data. Each unit of a Lazarus project will have a separate XML data file associated with it. Other documentation tools, such as Doc-O-Matic, require you to use formatted comments directly in your source code. The use of separate XML files keeps your code comments clean and easier to read and understand. The Lazarus project uses LazDE to create HTML pages that can be accessed at `http://lazarus-ccr.sourceforge.net/docs/lcl/`. It is planned that at a later time there will be an integrated help system in Lazarus itself that will use XML as the source for the documentation data. Current documentation of the XML datafiles can be found in the directory `[$LazDir]/docs/xml/`. The files located here are mostly empty skeleton files with little or no useful documentation. These files need to be adapted to be useful. To do this we need to open them in LazDE, but first we need to build the LazDE tool using the project that is provided.

To build LazDE, proceed with the following steps:

1. Using Lazarus **Project Wizard**, click on the **Open Project** button.
2. Browse the directory [$LazDir]/doceditor/.
3. Select the project file lazde.lpi.
4. Compile the project by clicking on *Ctrl + F9*.
5. Run the application.

If you are attempting to build the LazDE tool on a Linux-based system, you will either need to copy the doceditor directory to a different directory where you have read and write permission or change the permission of the existing doceditor directory and run Lazarus as root.

Examining existing source documentation

When you run the application, you should be presented with a window similar to the following screenshot:

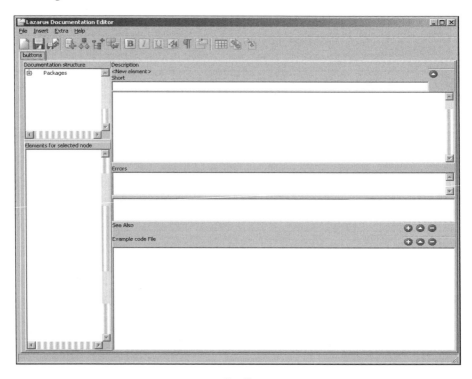

To become familiar with the LazDE tool, let us first open an existing documentation file.

1. Click on the **File** menu and choose **Open** from the submenu.

2. Browse to the directory in which Lazarus is installed, and select the /docs/ xml/lcl subdirectory.

3. Select the file buttons.xml and click on the **Open** button.

In the upper-left corner of the LazDE window is a treeview with the label **Documentation Structure**. You should now see a new node titled **Packages**. The steps to be followed are:

1. Click the plus sign next to the new node to expand it.

2. The node titled **lcl** is now visible. Expand this node.

3. Now the node titled **Buttons** is visible; click on this node title.

The treeview **Elements for selected node** will now populate with the names of constants, types, and classes defined in the buttons.xml unit, as seen in the following screenshot. Other units that use the buttons unit are also included as nodes of the **Buttons** root node.

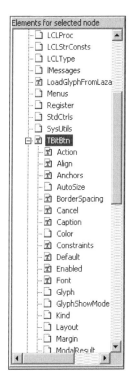

Select and expand the **TBitBtn** class node and you will notice that the properties of that class are added as subnodes. The glyphs of the **TBitBtn** node and other nodes have the letter T on them. These nodes are nodes that contain documentation for the class or property. Undocumented elements have a yellow glyph. Make sure the **TBitBtn** node is clicked; the window appears similar to the following screenshot:

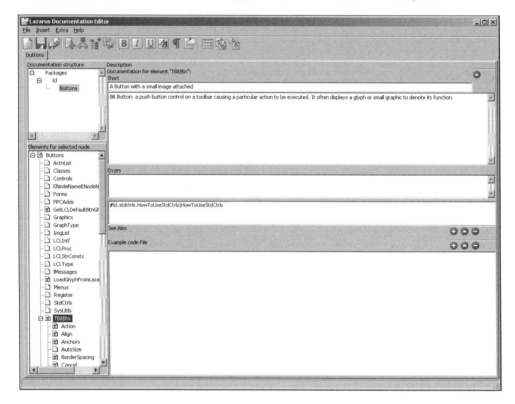

The **Short** description, main **Description**, and **See Also** fields are populated with information on the **TBitBtn** class. The **Short** description editbox is used to give a short explanation of what the class or property is. The memo field **Description** is used to provide a longer and more detailed description of the class or property. The **See Also** field is used to create links to other pages that are related to a class or property being documented. In the case of **TBitBtn**, there is a link to the documentation on using the StdCrls unit. This field is linked to three buttons that allow you to add, edit, or delete these linkages. The **Errors** field allows you to add information on the types of errors that a class or property can raise. The last field, **Example code File**, also allows you to add links to pages with examples of the usage of the class or property.

Documenting your code

Now that we have built LazDE and looked at a basic overview of the interface, let's document the code that we have created. Click on the **File** menu and select **New**. You will be presented with a dialog as shown in the following screenshot:

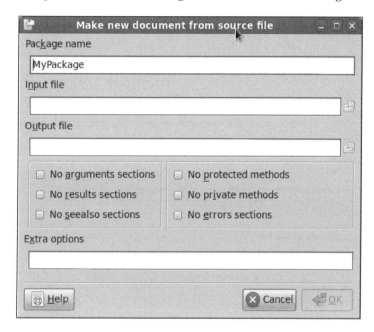

Create the new documentation package as follows:

1. Leave **Package name** as **MyPackage**.

2. Click on the icon after the **Input file** editbox and browse to the directory that includes the file DRU.pas, which we used previously in *Chapter 4, Converting Delphi*.

3. Click on the icon next to the **Output file** editbox, and select a directory to write to and call the output file MyDoc.xml.

The main application screen will appear and we can now begin documenting our unit. Let's do that by documenting the **tBtnRunClick** event as follows:

1. In the **Document Structure** window, expand all nodes until you reach the last node, titled **DRU**.

2. In the **Elements for selected node** treeview, scroll down and select the **tBtnRunClick** node.

3. In the **Short** description field, enter a brief description, such as: `This procedure is called when the tBtnRun button is clicked.`

4. In the main **Description** field, enter a more detailed description, such as: `This procedure is called when the tBtnRun button is clicked. It first updates the status bar of the application, detailing what delimiter will be replaced and what the new delimiter will be. It then calls the procedure ReplaceDelimiters, and finally updates the statusbar after completion with start time and end time.`

5. Since this procedure is associated with the **tBtnRun** button, let's make a link in the **See Also** field as follows:

    1. Click on the **Add** button next to the **See Also** field, and the dialog in the following screenshot will appear:

    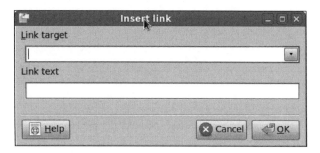

    2. Click on the drop-down arrow. Scroll through the content and select **TfrDRU.tBtnRun**.

    3. In the **Link text** field, enter `The Run Button`.

    4. Click on **OK**. The entry **TfrDRU.tBtnRun | BtnRun** is now added to the **See Also** field.

6. In the **Elements for selected node** treeview, click on the **tBtnRun** node.

7. In the **Short** description field, enter: `The user clicks on this button to execute the replacing of the delimiter.`

8. In the main **Description** field, enter: `After the user has set all the parameter of which character is to be used to replace the existing file delimiter as the new delimiter, the user clicks on this button to perform the substitution.`

Now that we have documented two of the elements, we can save the project and build our documentation.

1. Save the file by clicking on the blue-disk icon.

2. Click on the **Extra** menu and select **Build**. The dialog in the following screenshot will be presented:

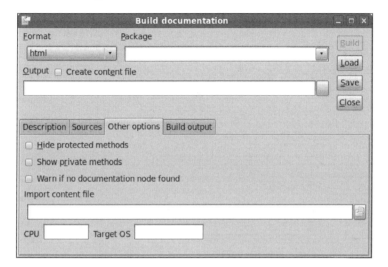

3. Click on the **Description** tab and then click on the **Add All** button.

4. Click on the **Sources** tab and then click on the **Add** button.

5. Browse to the directory containing the source files for our project and select the DRU.pas file.

6. In the **Package** drop-down box, select **MyDocs**.

7. Click on the button next to the **Output** editbox and select a directory where the output files will be created.

8. Click on **Build**.

The **Build output** tab will now become active, and you will see messages about the build process. The last message should be **Documentation successfully built**. You should now be able to open the output directory in your file browser and view the file index.html. Open this file in the browser of your choice and you can examine the documentation that you created.

This is the basic procedure for creating documentation using the LazDE tool. You can create more detailed documentation that uses graphs and tables in the main **Description** field by using the various icons on the LazDE toolbar. The LazDE tool is actually a GUI frontend to the Free Pascal command-line tool, FPDoc.

Using FPDoc

FPDoc is the command-line tool that is used to combine Pascal source file units and XML-formatted documentation files to create reference documentation in a variety of formats. FPDoc can create documentation in the following formats:

- HTML: HTML with Style Sheets and JavaScript. JavaScript is used to create the class properties and class method window.
- XHTML: It is a stricter HTML syntax.
- LaTeX: It generates LaTeX files that can be used to create Postscript or PDF. Free Pascal provides the `fpc.sty` file for use with LaTeX.
- Text: It includes plain ASCII text files. There's no cross-referencing.
- Man: Unix man pages. For each function, procedure, and method identifier, a separate man page is created. Separate units are created for constants, types, variables, and resource strings.
- CHM: It is a compressed HTML file. It is compressed using `lzx` compression.
- RTF: It stands for Rich Text Format files.

FPDoc has many command-line options, including the following:

- `input`: This is the name of the Pascal source file that will be scanned to create a skeleton description file. This option can be given multiple times.
- `descr`: This is the name of the description file (`.xml` file) that contains the documentation for the units supplied in the input option.
- `format`: This is the output format of the documentation. The following options are valid:
    - `htm`: It includes plain HTML files with 8.3-conforming filenames
    - `html`: It includes HTML files with long filenames
    - `xhtml`: It includes XHTML files with long filenames
    - `latex`: It includes LaTeX files, which uses the `fpc.sty` style
    - `xml`: It includes structured XML files
    - `chm`: It includes compressed HTML files

- `package`: This is the name of the package that is being documented. It is also used as the default output option.

- `output`: This is the output filename; no extension is to be given. If not given, the output is written to the standard output.

The simplest command line to generate code can be as follows:

```
fpdoc --package=mypackage --input=mycode.pp
```

This will scan `mycode.pp` and create skeleton documentation and write the output to the directory `mypackage`.

Let's now use our previous example of the `DRU.pas` file documentation with FPDoc to create a more complete command-line example.

```
fpdoc --package=DRU --input=DRU.pas --desrc=dru.xml --format=html
--output=MyDRUDocumentation
```

This will create new documentation in the `MyDRUDocumentation` directory by reading the `DRU.pas` file to create a skeleton documentation file. The documentation from the `dru.xml` file will be used to complete the skeleton file. The output will be written as HTML.

For more information on using FPDoc, see the reference manual at the following link:

```
http://www.freepascal.org/docs-html/fpdoc/fpdoc.html#fpdocli1.html
```

Summary

In this chapter we learned how to document our source code using the Lazarus Documentation Editor tool, LazDE.

We built the LazDE tool, noting that, if doing so on Linux, we may have problems unless we copy the source to a new directory, change permissions, or build the project using the root account.

We opened the existing Lazarus documentation file for the `TButton` unit and examined the `TBitBtn` class. We saw that nodes in the element listing that contain existing documentation can be identified by their icons. We looked at the different fields for providing descriptions of classes or methods, listing possible errors raised, and linking classes or methods to one another.

We created documentation for the DRU project form we created in *Chapter 4, Converting a Delphi Program*, by adding documentation to the procedure called when clicking on the **Run** button and briefly documenting the **Run** button itself. Then, we built the documentation as HTML files and opened the output in a browser.

Finally, we looked at the FPDoc command-line tool, which is actually called by LazDE to create documentation. We looked at some of the command line options needed to create documentation. We learned that FPDoc is capable of generating documentation in different formats, such as HTML, CHM, and LaTeX.

In the final chapter we will learn how to rebuild Lazarus with a different toolkit.

7
Rebuilding Lazarus with a GTK2 Interface

The Lazarus integrated development environment supports a number of graphical widget sets such as GTK2 and QT on Windows, Linux, and Mac OS X. Win32 and Win64 widget sets are supported on the various versions of Windows. The Carbon widget set is supported on Mac OS X. Cocoa support is in the alpha stages for Mac OS X. Custom Drawn Controls support is also in the alpha stage. The Lazarus interface can be rebuilt using any of the supported widget sets. Choosing a widget set with alpha support may lead to an unstable build. In this chapter we will learn to rebuild the Lazarus interface with the GTK2 toolkit on a Windows platform.

Rebuilding Lazarus interface on Windows

Before you rebuild Lazarus on a Windows platform, you need to install the GTK2 libraries for Windows. You can download the current version installers from one of the following locations:

- `http://www.gtk.org/download/win32.php`, for Win32
- `http://www.gtk.org/download/win64.php`, for Win64

The Windows 64-bit version of the GTK libraries is considered to be experimental at this time.

You can choose to download individual packages or download them all in one bundle. You can read the documentation on the page for more information on installing the individual packages; otherwise, find the **all-in-one** bundle, download it, and follow the instructions for installing.

Before rebuilding the Lazarus interface, click on **Help** in the menu and select **About Lazarus,** and you will see the dialog as shown in the following screenshot:

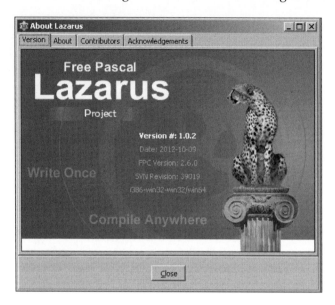

Notice the line **i386-win32-win32/win64**; this is the current interface widget type.

To start the rebuilding process, click on **Tools** in the main menu and select **Configure "Build Lazarus"**.

The dialog that is presented to you allows you to set the options for rebuilding Lazarus. Set the options as follows:

1.   Set the **Profile to build** drop-down box to **Optimized IDE**.
2.   Set **LCL widget type** to **gtk 2**.
3.   Set **Target OS** to **Win32** or **Win64**, depending on your platform version.
4.   Set **Target CPU** to **i386** or **x86_64**.

The **Options** field has been been populated with the value **-O2 -g- -Xs** since **Optimized IDE** was selected as the profile. Click on the **Build** button to start the rebuilding process. During the build process, the **Messages** window will display information on the progress of the build. Once the build is complete, Lazarus will restart. Does the Lazarus interface look different? Since we haven't changed the gtk theme, it probably looks as if nothing happened. Click on **Help** from the main menu and select **About Lazarus,** and you will see the dialog as shown in the following screenshot:

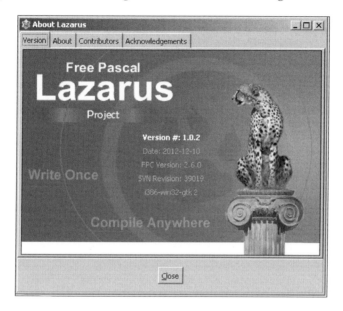

Notice that the widget type is now **i386-win32-gtk 2**.

You can change the gtk theme by creating the file gtkrc in the subdirectory /etc/ gtk-2.0 of the directory in which you installed the gtk. In that file, add the line, gtk-theme-name = "Emacs".

Restart Lazarus and you should notice a slight difference in the look. Open or start a new project and you should notice that the icons in the **Code Explorer**, **Project Inspector**, and **Object Inspector** windows are different. You can use this method to rebuild Lazarus with any of the supported widget sets you like.

Summary

In this chapter we learned the process of rebuilding the Lazarus interface with a widget type other than the default Windows widget type, which uses the gtk libraries.

We downloaded and installed the **all-in-one** bundle of the gtk library for Windows and noted that it is possible to download the individual components of the library, if desired.

We rebuilt the Lazarus interface using the **Configure Build Lazarus** options in the **Tools** menu and set the profile to optimize the IDE build.

Once the interface was rebuilt, we learned how to set the gtk theme by creating the gtkrc file.

Index

P

PrepareItem method 79
Project Options dialog, Source
    Editor Window 23, 25
property editors 76

Q

QT 7
quick icons, Source Editor Window 23

R

Red Hat Package Management.
    See RPM format
RegisterComponentEditor 78
RegisterComponents 71
Rich Text Format (RTF) 90
RPM format 6
rtfpars 50
Run menu, Source Editor Window 25-27
Run-Time Library (RTL) 7
Run To Cursor command 43

S

sh_pas 50
sh_xml 50
source documentation
  examining 84-86
Source Editor window
  about 18, 22
  Common Control tab 28
  Data Controls tab 29
  Dialogs tab 29
  LCL Palette 27
  LCL Palette window 23
  main menu 23
  Projects Options dialog 23, 25
  quick icons 23
  Run menu 25, 26, 27
  SQLdb tab 29
  Standard tab 27

SQLdb tab, Source Editor Window
  about 29
  TMySQL50Connection 30
  TODBCConnection 30
  TOracleConnection 30
  TSQLite3Connection 30
  TSQLQuery 29
  TSQLTransaction 29
Standard tab, Source Editor Window
  about 27
  TBitButton 28
  TFrame 28
  TGroupBox 28
  TMainMenu 27
  TNoteBook 28
  TPopupMenu 27
  TSpeedButton 28
  TStringGrid 28
  TToggleBox 28
Step Into command 43
Step Over command 43
Stop command 43
Subversion (SVN) 14
SVN repositories 14

T

TAfterWriteMsgEvent 75
TBaseComponentEditor 78
TBeforeWriteMsgEvent 75, 76
TBitButton 28
TCheckListBox component editor 79
TClassPropertyEditor 77
TComponentEditor 78
TCustomTreeView.DefaultItems 53
TCustomTreeView.ExpandSignType 53
TCustomTreeView.OnSelectionChange
    event 53
TCustomTreeView.Options property 52
TCustomTreeView.Options property,
    options
  tvoAllowMultiselect 52
  tvoAutoExpand 52
  tvoAutoInsertMark 52
  tvoAutoItemHeight 52

Thank you for buying
Getting Started With Lazarus IDE

About Packt Publishing

Packt, pronounced 'packed', published its first book "*Mastering phpMyAdmin for Effective MySQL Management*" in April 2004 and subsequently continued to specialize in publishing highly focused books on specific technologies and solutions.

Our books and publications share the experiences of your fellow IT professionals in adapting and customizing today's systems, applications, and frameworks. Our solution based books give you the knowledge and power to customize the software and technologies you're using to get the job done. Packt books are more specific and less general than the IT books you have seen in the past. Our unique business model allows us to bring you more focused information, giving you more of what you need to know, and less of what you don't.

Packt is a modern, yet unique publishing company, which focuses on producing quality, cutting-edge books for communities of developers, administrators, and newbies alike. For more information, please visit our website: www.packtpub.com.

About Packt Open Source

In 2010, Packt launched two new brands, Packt Open Source and Packt Enterprise, in order to continue its focus on specialization. This book is part of the Packt Open Source brand, home to books published on software built around Open Source licences, and offering information to anybody from advanced developers to budding web designers. The Open Source brand also runs Packt's Open Source Royalty Scheme, by which Packt gives a royalty to each Open Source project about whose software a book is sold.

Writing for Packt

We welcome all inquiries from people who are interested in authoring. Book proposals should be sent to author@packtpub.com. If your book idea is still at an early stage and you would like to discuss it first before writing a formal book proposal, contact us; one of our commissioning editors will get in touch with you.

We're not just looking for published authors; if you have strong technical skills but no writing experience, our experienced editors can help you develop a writing career, or simply get some additional reward for your expertise.

NetBeans IDE 7 Cookbook

ISBN: 978-1-849512-50-3   Paperback: 308 pages

Over 70 highly focused practicle recipes to maximize your output with NetBeans

1. Covers the full spectrum of features offered by the NetBeans IDE

2. Discover ready-to-implement solutions for developing desktop and web applications

3. Learn how to deploy, debug, and test your software using NetBeans IDE

Xcode 4 iOS Development Beginner's Guide

ISBN: 978-1-849691-30-7   Paperback: 432 pages

Use the powerful Xcode 4 suite of tools to build applications for the iPhone and iPad from scratch

1. Learn how to use Xcode 4 to build simple, yet powerful applications with ease

2. Each chapter builds on what you have learned already

3. Learn to add audio and video playback to your applications

4. Plentiful step-by-step examples, images, and diagrams to get you up to speed in no time with helpful hints along the way

Please check **www.PacktPub.com** for information on our titles

PUBLISHING

open source *
community experience distilled

PHPEclipse: A User Guide

ISBN: 978-1-904811-44-2   Paperback: 228 pages

Use the leading open source integrated developement environment to develop, organize, and debug your PHP web development projects

1. Compact guide to using Eclipse and PHPEclipse for web development

2. Slash development time by improving the efficiency of your PHP coding and organizing your projects in the PHPEclipse environment

3. Learn to use Eclipse for debugging PHP applications, interfacing with databases, and managing source code

Aptana RadRails: An IDE for Rails Development

ISBN: 978-1-847193-98-8   Paperback: 248 pages

A comprehensive guide to using RaidRails to develop your Ruby on Rails project in a professional and productive manner

1. Comprehensive guide to using RadRails during the whole development cycle

2. Code Assistance, Graphical Debugger, Testing, Integrated Console

3. Manage your gems, plug-ins, servers, generators, and Rake tasks

Please check **www.PacktPub.com** for information on our titles

5270105R00066

Printed in Great Britain
by Amazon.co.uk, Ltd.,
Marston Gate.